Bruce Springsteen

BORN IN THE U.S.A.

Bruce Springsteen
BORN IN THE U.S.A.

TEXT BY
ROBERT HILBURN

Rolling Stone

A ROLLING STONE PRESS BOOK
SIDGWICK & JACKSON LONDON

First Published in 1985 in Great Britain by
Sidgwick and Jackson Limited

Originally published in the United States of America by
Charles Scribner's Sons, 115 Fifth Avenue, New York,
NY 10003

Art Direction by Howard Klein

ISBN 0-283-99314-6 (hardcover)
ISBN 0-283-99325-1 (softcover)

Printed in Great Britain by
Butler and Tanner Limited, Frome, Somerset
for Sidgwick and Jackson Limited, 1 Tavistock Chambers,
Bloomsbury Way, London WC1A 2SG

Photo editor: Amanda Joy Rubin

ACKNOWLEDGMENTS

•

ROBERT HILBURN WOULD LIKE TO THANK: TIM McGINNIS, A SENSITIVE AND ASTUTE EDITOR WHO REALLY LISTENS TO THE MUSIC; CHRISTOPHER CONNELLY, WHOSE SUGGESTIONS PROVIDED SOME SPIRIT IN THE NIGHT TO PARTS OF THE MANUSCRIPT; THOSE WHOSE FRIENDSHIP IS SURELY A COMFORT TO SPRINGSTEEN: JON LANDAU, STEVE VAN ZANDT, PETER PHILBIN, JIMMY IOVINE, DAVE MARSH, BARBARA CARR, AND THOSE WHOSE SUPPORT IS A BLESSING TO ME: KATHI BARR AND A SLEW OF HILBURNS: ROB, KATHY, MONTGOMERY, JOHN AND ALICE MARIE. ALSO: BRUCE SPRINGSTEEN, FOR TAKING TIME—ONCE AGAIN.

THE EDITORS OF ROLLING STONE PRESS ARE GRATEFUL FOR THE CONTRIBUTIONS OF HOWARD KLEIN, MICHAEL PIETSCH, FRANK SPOTNITZ, DEBORAH MITCHELL, MARY ASTADOURIAN, AMANDA RUBIN, SANDRA HIGASHI, HOWARD B. LIEBOWITZ, CHRISTOPHER CONNELLY AND *BACKSTREETS* MAGAZINE.

•

THE Bottom LINE

p

ALLAN PEPPER & STANLEY SNADOWSKY

15 WEST FOURTH STREET, NEW YORK, NEW YORK 10012

$5.00

August 17, 1975

AN EVENING

BRUCE SPRI

& THE E STE

Creative reigns in rock & roll are notoriously brief. Elvis Presley's most influential records were all made in the three years that ended with the release of "Jailhouse Rock" in 1956. Though he continued to exercise his questioning spirit, Bob Dylan never regained his hold on the rock audience after his motorcycle accident of 1966. The Beatles burned out before the start of the 1970s.

A decade after he was featured on the covers of *Time* and *Newsweek* in 1975, Bruce Springsteen was still reaching for his artistic and commercial peak. The most acclaimed figure in American rock by the time his album *The River* was released in 1980, Springsteen has added to both his art and his audience with his two subsequent LPs. *Nebraska*, a stark, compassionate look at loss of hope in America, dazzled critics and listeners in 1982. In 1984 *Born in the U.S.A.* spread Springsteen's hard-times portraits and personal celebrations to a huge new audience.

By the time he and the E Street Band reached Greensboro, North Carolina, in January 1985, Springsteen was halfway through an international tour that would be seen by an estimated four million people. *Born in the U.S.A.* had sold five million copies—almost double his previous high with *Born to Run*—and had just regained the Number One position on the national sales charts.

It was Springsteen's first local appearance in four years, and tickets for both shows at the 15,500-seat Greensboro Coliseum had sold out as fast as the box office could collect the money. Fans draped welcoming banners over the balcony rails ("Ooh, ooh, we gotta crush on you") and shouted his name after almost every song.

For more than three hours, Springsteen performed with an intensity that challenged both his stamina and the audience's ability to absorb. Rather than the narrow range offered in most pop music performances, Springsteen's embraced many styles and emotions—from the youthful exhilaration of his *Born to Run* days to the darker social realism of his recent work.

His fans have always been thrilled by Springsteen's energy and drive, and the Greensboro concert was no exception. But now what they seem to treasure most is his emotional honesty and integrity.

"You can't live on what you did yesterday or what's going to happen tomorrow," he told me in 1980. "If you fall into that trap, you don't belong on stage. That's what rock & roll is: a promise, an oath. It's about being as true as you can at any particular moment."

Springsteen's biggest triumph is that he has lived up to his own oath. In an age that has taught us to expect corruption and compromise, he invites trust. He has made it possible once again to put faith in a rock & roll singer.

It's dangerous to attribute anything as complex as Springsteen's motivation to a single incident or person, but there's reason to believe that much of what makes Springsteen run is based on his perception of his own first and greatest hero, Elvis Presley. After his split with Mike Appel, the aggressive ex-Marine who had managed his career for the four years climaxed by the release of *Born to Run,* Springsteen addressed the dangers of fame in these terms: "Mike Appel thought he would be Colonel Parker and I'd be Elvis. Only he wasn't Colonel Parker and I wasn't Elvis."

Elvis played an important part in the conversation the first time I met Springsteen, in 1974. Though he had built a reputation around his native New Jersey, Springsteen was largely unknown on the West Coast at the time of the interview. He and the E Street Band weren't even headliners yet. They had opened that night at the Santa Monica Civic Auditorium for Dr. John, the growly-voiced rock & blues piano player from New Orleans. But you could see that things were beginning to change for Springsteen, and he was trying to figure out how to adjust. His two Columbia albums were critically acclaimed, and his record company was promoting him aggressively.

On this evening, he was uncomfortable talking about himself. The only time he relaxed was when he spoke about Elvis.

"Before rock & roll, I didn't have any purpose. I tried to play football and baseball and all those things...and I just didn't fit. I was running through a maze. It was never a hobby. It was a reason to live. It was the only one I had. It was kind of life or death."

Bruce was eight years old when he saw Elvis on the *Ed Sullivan Show* in 1957, and Elvis became a symbol of freedom and future to a youngster from a New Jersey town that seemed a storage house for compromise and failure. When he saw Elvis, Bruce decided that's what he would be when he grew up.

In the Greensboro Coliseum in 1985, Springsteen was still talking about Elvis. Only this time his tone was different. Early in the concert, he told about driving by Graceland in 1976. Springsteen laughed as he recalled how he climbed the wall and raced to Elvis' front door, hoping to get a chance to meet him. He was caught and turned away by the guards with no sight of Elvis.

He then described his feelings when he learned that Elvis had died. "It was hard to understand how somebody whose music took away so many people's loneliness could have ended up as lonely as he did." Springsteen began singing "Bye, Bye Johnny," a song he wrote shortly after Presley's death. It's a mournful tune that ends, "You didn't have to die, you didn't have to die."

Presley's death in some ways made an even stronger impression on Springsteen than the rock star's music had. Elvis' decline was a warning and a challenge. If the young Elvis was a compelling symbol of the possible, the older Elvis was a sign of the tragedy that could accompany the realization of your dreams.

This posed some questions for Bruce: What if you remained true to the rock & roll ideal? How far could you take it? Was it possible to avoid the indifference and indulgence that eventually sabotaged the artistic vision of so many other rock heroes?

When he returned later for an encore, Springsteen performed a tender, acoustic version of "Can't Help Falling in Love," one of Elvis' trademark ballads. Springsteen's voice doesn't have the purity of Presley's but there was a touching sweetness in his rendition. Before the applause died, the rest of the E Street Band moved into place, and Springsteen tore into the most rousing version of "Born to Run" I've heard in the dozens of times I've seen him perform. The song is Springsteen's greatest expression of determination and hope. But on this night, it seemed to have an undercurrent of rage, as if Springsteen were reminding himself and everyone present that what happened to Elvis wasn't inevitable.

In the dressing room after the Greensboro concert, Springsteen reflected on maintaining balance in a field littered with failures.

"The casualty rate in this business is real high," he acknowledged. "But life is a struggle for most people. It's a thin line between surviving and not making it. It's like people with their finger in the dike, trying to hold back the flood all the time. That's what our band is about.

"The shows aren't a casual thing, even though they are filled with fun and wildness. There should be beauty, but there's also got to be ugliness and brutality. If you don't have all of that in the evening, you're not doing it. If you turn away, that's the beginning of the end. That's what you spend your time doing—trying not to turn away."

1 Childhood is a time of immense hopes and insecurities, and the neighborhoods of your childhood chronicle those emotions better than a diary. Old street corners and playgrounds remind you of early aspirations and doubts, setbacks and successes. John Lennon said he felt psychologically naked when he went back to Liverpool or bumped into one of the old gang. "That's one time when you can't hide from yourself. The records, the fame—none of it shields you. You remember exactly who you are deep inside."

Maybe that's why Bruce Springsteen finds it hard to shake a sentimental attachment to his home town—even though he spent much of his New Jersey school days yearning to get away from places like Asbury Park and Freehold. Familiar streets and faces provide an emotional anchor that can be a useful balance against the pressures of the pop spotlight, and Springsteen values that protective balance.

"One of the things that was always on my mind to do was to maintain connections with the people I'd grown up with, and the sense of the community where I came from," he said shortly after the start of the Born in the U.S.A. tour. "That's why I stayed in New Jersey. The danger of fame is in forgetting or being distracted."

Someone who has worked closely with Springsteen for years told me, "There's always part of him back home. He needs to go back there and check up on himself. I remember one night he drove me all through that area for three hours. He'd point out places and tell me some little story about something that happened there."

Most people think of Asbury Park, the seedy beachfront town on the Jersey shore, as Springsteen's home town. His debut album was called *Greetings from Asbury Park, N.J.*, and he often tells stories on stage about the years he spent there, playing clubs and trying to put his rock & roll dreams in place. But Bruce was born eighteen miles away in Freehold, New Jersey. Both of these Central Jersey towns—about an hour's drive from Manhattan or Philadelphia—take pride in their past. Asbury Park was once a thriving resort with luxury hotels and a busy boardwalk. Freehold was the site of an important battle during the Revolutionary War; there's still a museum in town with artifacts from the battle.

There's not as much to say about these towns' futures. You can picture a young Bruce walking along Main Street and out on Highway 9, ducking into the sandwich shop here and the dime store there, daydreaming about the escape that he would eventually glamorize in "Thunder Road" and "Born to Run." But the thing that strikes you about this area now is the emptiness. Walking through Freehold is like walking through any of a hundred American towns that have been strangled by changing times.

Asbury Park is more depressing than Freehold. You don't have to go to the edges of this town to find the darkness. The boardwalk—the heart of Asbury Park—was all but deserted during the two days I spent there in the summer of 1984. That day, the only sounds in the once-proud convention center were electronic zaps from a lone

"All my houses seem to have been way stations." Overleaf: The Asbury Park boardwalk, still waiting for news of the "recovery."

video game. A boy and his dog had the entire beach to themselves. Most of the attractions that lured people to Asbury Park were destroyed in a race riot more than a decade ago. There's talk about a redevelopment project to save the town, but the smart money is headed south to Atlantic City and all the new casinos.

•

THEY'RE CLOSING DOWN THE TEXTILE MILL ACROSS FROM THE RAILROAD TRACKS. FOREMAN SAYS THESE JOBS ARE GOING BOYS AND THEY AIN'T COMING BACK.

"MY HOMETOWN"

•

A few blocks away from the boardwalk, John Eddie, a young rocker who was causing a stir in the region that summer, was setting up his equipment at the Stone Pony, a club Springsteen frequently visits when he's in town.

"I think this whole area's lucky to have Bruce, especially the young people. They need something to look up to. You can see this town is beat."

"It's strange. Go a few miles one way and you've got millionaires

Below: St. Rose of Lima in Freehold, N.J. where Springsteen attended grade school. He was hard pressed to remember any good times. Right: Public high school. The yearbook tag for the self-described loner was "Bruce." Overleaf: The house on South Street where Springsteen spent most of his childhood.

walking along the boardwalk. Go a few miles the other way and you've got beautiful homes, but this place is something else. You get the feeling that the life has been sucked out of Asbury Park. It's like something from a horror novel."

Things seem more pleasant on the surface in Freehold, the county seat of Monmouth County. There's a small-town calmness that turns out, once you've been there a while, to be simply uneventfulness. Many of the young people of Freehold sense the emptiness and leave as soon as they get out of school, but a core of residents hang on. It's as if the old people in the borough have lived there so long that they don't know what they'd do somewhere else.

"I come from an area where there was not a lot of success," Springsteen once said. "I didn't know anyone who made a record before me. I didn't know anybody who had made anything."

He also said, "It was a real classic little town, very intent on maintaining the status quo. Everything was looked at as a threat. Kids were looked at as a nuisance and a threat."

One of the few things that Freehold has to speak proudly of is Springsteen. When I visited Liverpool in 1983, I found a lot of resentment toward the Beatles from people who never forgave them for moving to London after they became successful. But Freehold— and all of Jersey—is full of affection for Springsteen. One reason is that Bruce still lives in the area, even if it is in a million dollar home twenty minutes away in Rumson. They're also proud that Springsteen fans from around the world travel to Freehold and Asbury Park the way Beatles fans visit Liverpool and Elvis fans make pilgrimages to Memphis.

The Stone Pony is where most of the fans end up. Near a bar at the rear of the club, there's a collage of photos: Springsteen huddles with fans in one series, plays softball in another.

"People come here from all over the country hoping to see Bruce," explained the Stone Pony's manager, Butch Pielka. "If he's not here that night, they just take pictures of the club or something. It's not like there's a Springsteen museum. So this is the only place they know to go."

Springsteen is such an inspiration to young people throughout the state that bills were entered in the state legislature nominating "Born to Run" as the official state song.

What a great move. Too great, in fact, not to botch up. The bills were voted down. In what New Jersey textbooks may eventually describe as the great Springsteen compromise, the lawmakers finally agreed to declare "Born to Run" the state's "unofficial youth song." Some assemblymen argued that the song's lyrics set a bad example, that all the references to running away encouraged young people to flee the realities of life. In his own defense, Springsteen told *Musician* magazine in 1984, "To me, there was an aspect of [escape], but I always felt it was more about searching."

Bruce Frederick Springsteen was born on September 23, 1949, the first of three children for Douglas and Adele Springsteen. The family name is Dutch, but there's Irish blood on his father's side and

The old Freehold neighborhood—"Liverpool" for Springsteen fans.

his mother's family is Italian.

See Bruce's parents at one of his concerts and you can pick up immediately on the differences in personality. His dad is short and squat, and he looks a bit too intimidating for anyone to walk up and say hello to. Part of it is that he's shy, but there is also the reserve of a headstrong man who felt cheated for so long by life that he now finds it hard, even with his son's success, to open up.

Adele, however, jumps about like a cheerleader at the start of every song, hugging fans who stop by to say hello. She has maintained a scrapbook on Bruce ever since the days of Steel Mill, one of his first bands. Shortly after I wrote a review of *Born to Run* in 1975, I received a letter from Mrs. Springsteen:

My husband and I want to thank you very much for the article on Bruce. Naturally, we are keeping a scrapbook and all goes in, good and bad . . . All the publicity Bruce has been getting is unbelievable, especially the cover stories on *Time* and *Newsweek*. We are very proud of him and know he can handle it all. We went to see Bruce play in Oakland and it was a night we will always remember. Bill Graham had undershirts with the cover picture of *Time* and *Newsweek* (*Time* on the front, *Newsweek* on the back).

Douglas and Adele, who met each other in Freehold, were married in 1948 and lived briefly in an apartment before moving in with Douglas's parents. That house—where Bruce was born—was torn down years ago and the land is now covered by a church parking lot. Bruce's father had various jobs, including stints as a factory worker and a prison guard. But mostly he drove a bus. Adele worked as a secretary for a land title company. The family lived briefly in a house on Institute Street that is shown on the lyric sheet for *Born in the U.S.A.*, in a photo of Springsteen leaning against a tree in the front yard. The main Springsteen residence was one side of a two-story, two-family house next to Ducky Slattery's Sinclair Station on South Street.

The house was just a couple of blocks from Freehold's downtown area and close to St. Rose of Lima, the parochial school that Bruce attended. He later went to Freehold Regional High School and took a few classes at Ocean County Community College, where he was encouraged to be a writer. But Springsteen had made up his mind early that he wanted to be a musician.

Bruce can even point to the night he made the decision. He was so excited in 1957 when he saw Elvis on the *Ed Sullivan Show* that he asked his mother for a guitar. She got him one, but also made him take lessons, which he hated so much that he put the guitar away. It wasn't until the Beatles arrived in 1964 that he tried the guitar again, buying one in a pawn shop for $18. The hours he spent in his room, listening to records and learning to play, were a constant source of tension between Bruce and his father, who wanted to see him pursue a more practical career.

By most accounts Bruce was a loner—not a flashy rebel, but still rigidly independent. Diane Forman, a high school classmate of

Steel Mill's guitar hero with regulation 1969 hair length.

Springsteen, remembers Bruce as a "real quiet boy, not someone who made a big impression on you." In a 1984 interview, she added, "He's around town a lot, but he keeps to himself. I think it makes him feel uncomfortable when people make a big deal over him. I remember seeing him at the high school football game a few years ago. He was just standing there, and no one realized who he was. Then someone recognized him and he was gone."

About his school days, Springsteen has said, "I didn't even make it to class clown. I had nowhere near that amount of notoriety. I didn't have. . .the flair to be the complete jerk. It was like I didn't exist. It was the wall, then me. But I was working on the inside all the time. A lot of rock & roll people went through this solitary existence.

"If you're gonna be good at something, you've gotta be alone a lot to practice. There has to be a certain involuntariness to it. Like my youngest sister, she could play if she wanted to. But she's too pretty. She's popular, you know what I mean? It's like simple as that. She ain't gonna sit in the house in her room no eight a hours a day and play the piano. No way."

Springsteen was so uncomfortable at school that he skipped his own high school graduation.

One of the school's teachers thought Springsteen's long hair was disrespectful, so she appealed to his classmates. If they let him go through the graduation lines with hair that long, she said, they would be telling the whole community that a high school degree wasn't worth respect. No one came to Bruce's aid.

Springsteen saw a world beyond Freehold, and he began to reach for it as soon as he got access to a car. With a buddy or by himself, he used to sleep on the beach or head up to New York City. The Port Authority police would sometimes pick him up and call home. His mom used to come get him because his father refused to. Once he was home, however, his father was waiting.

In a famous rap during the Born to Run tour, he told the story; "I used to slick my hair back real tight so he couldn't tell how long it was gettin'. And try to sneak through the kitchen. But the old man, he'd catch me every night and drag me back into the kitchen. He'd

Route 9, the escape route out of Freehold.

make me sit down at the table in the dark, and he would sit there tellin' me… In the wintertime, he used to turn on the gas stove and close all the doors so it got real hot in there. And I can remember just sittin' there in the dark, him tellin' me, tellin' me, tellin' me… And I could always hear that voice, no matter how long I sat there. But I could never, ever see his face."

Springsteen now dismisses many of those early tensions as typical of the strains most young people experience. But the attempts by family, school and the church to break his independent spirit seemed only to toughen him.

Some of his most emotional songs—"Adam Raised a Cain," "Factory," "Independence Day"—would deal with his relationship with his father. He loved his father, but hated what he felt had happened to him. He remembers the day one of his aunts showed him a photo of his dad just after coming back from World War II.

"He looked just like John Garfield in this great suit, he looked like he was gonna eat the photographer's head off," Bruce said. "I couldn't ever remember him looking that proud or that defiant when I was growing up. I used to wonder what happened to all that pride, how it turned into so much bitterness. He had been so disappointed, had so much stuff beaten out of him by then…that he couldn't accept the idea that I had a dream and I had possibilities. The things I wanted, he thought were just foolish."

•

DADDY WORKED HIS WHOLE LIFE, FOR
   NOTHING BUT PAIN
NOW HE WALKS THESE EMPTY ROOMS,
   LOOKING FOR SOMETHING TO BLAME
YOU INHERIT THE SINS, YOU INHERIT THE
   FLAMES,
ADAM RAISED A CAIN.

•

Through those early years, rock & roll was his ally. "I just know that when I started to play, it was like a gift. I started to feel alive. It was like some little guy stumbling down the street and finding a key. Rock & roll was the only thing I ever liked about myself."

Besides Elvis and the Beatles, Bruce loved the classic Top 40 rockers: the lonesome romanticism of Roy Orbison, the exuberance of Gary U.S. Bonds, the sensual exhortations of the Rolling Stones, the sweeping innocence of Phil Spector's hits, the Animals' urgency.

He would sit in his room, listening to the radio and trying to play his guitar along with the songs. He may have dreamed about being in a band, but for a long time he didn't make any moves to join or start one.

"Bruce didn't have any time for girls or sports," said George Theiss, the leader of Springsteen's first group, the Castiles. Theiss had a crush on Springsteen's sister Ginny, and he remembers going over to the house and finding Springsteen alone in his room. "He used to sit upstairs and play all the time. He was really dedicated."

Figuring he'd have an excuse to spend more time around Ginny if Springsteen were in his band, Theiss asked Bruce if he wanted to join the Castiles. The band's manager was impressed by Springsteen's guitar playing and added him to the group. Bruce was fifteen.

Over the next few months, the quintet played everything from supermarket openings and junior high school dances to roller rinks and drive-in theaters. Theiss handled most of the lead vocals, but Bruce took over on a couple of numbers, including the Who's "My Generation." The Castiles' appearance, as shown in publicity photos from those days: a sort of wimpy Beatles look, including frilly white shirts, black vests, dark pants, Beatle boots and longish, modified Beatle haircuts.

By 1967 they were playing bars throughout New Jersey, and they even got some dates in New York's Greenwich Village. But the Castiles couldn't get a record contract, and the group eventually dissolved. The music scene was changing. There was increasing demand for heavier, bluesier, Cream-influenced psychedelic sounds. This was guitar players' music, and a natural attraction for Springsteen. His next band, Earth, was in that mold.

Another factor was also at work: Springsteen outgrew the Castiles. "When I started, I wanted to play rhythm guitar," he once explained, "Just stand back and play rhythm; no singing or anything. But I found out I knew a little more than I thought. . .more than other guys that were in the band."

George Theiss, leader of the Castiles, is still pursuing his own rock & roll dreams. The day in 1984 when I met him he talked warmly of nights in the clubs when one of his bands really gets to the crowd. But there is also a lot of sadness. In his mid-thirties, Theiss works as a carpenter by day and tries to rehearse at night with another group.

Theiss put a record that he had financed himself on the turntable. The song wasn't distinctive, but his voice was pleasant enough to picture him, with the right breaks, having a hit some day. But he feels time is running out for him. He spoke about all the near misses over the years, and of the difficulties of keeping bands together when there isn't enough money for the band members not to take day jobs. As he spoke I wondered how he could go through years of rejection and still hold onto his dreams. I tried to find some diplomatic way to ask if it might not be more merciful just to give up the dream.

He rejected the question. "You can't stop trying and say, 'Well, I gave it my best,' because my best may not be until next year. Music is the best thing I can do. How can you walk away from that?"

Theiss's wife, Diana, sees in Springsteen's songs a lot of the Freehold people Bruce knew. "The thing that separates him from the rest of us is that he made it out," she said. "But I could see that he would make it. He was so dedicated."

Without bitterness, she added, "I remember being outside a club years ago and I had Justin [their son] in a backpack. Bruce pointed to us and told George, 'You're not going to make it with them.'

"He wasn't trying to be mean, he was just pointing out how much dedication it takes."

SUNSHINE IN

and GREAT BEAST presen

R. ZOOM and the SONIC BOOM

with BRUCE SPRINGSTEEN
and SUNNY JIM

SPECIAL
DDED GROUP **CORNERSTONE**

ONE BIG SHOW
RI. EVE. MAY 14, 8:30 PM
admission 2.50

One of rock's primary lures has always been its sense of celebration. As a tonic for doubts and frustrations, the music's boldest figures have offered optimism and release, challenge and inspiration. Elvis Presley, Chuck Berry, Little Richard and Jerry Lee Lewis offered both rebellion and inspiration to the generation of young people looking for rallying points in the rapidly changing social structure of the mid-'50s. The same liberating process was repeated in the '60s, when the Beatles, Bob Dylan, the Rolling Stones and Jimi Hendrix chipped away at social, political, sexual and racial attitudes of the day. These were bold, aggressive heroes whose achievements gave confidence and aspirations to their audiences.

In the '70s rock & roll lost some of its individualism and ability to inspire. Though numerous artists—Neil Young, Van Morrison, David Bowie, Lou Reed—contributed passionate, insightful works, the decade was dominated by "Saturday Night Fever" and a glut of loud, same-sounding "arena" bands whose records sold hugely but lacked new ideas. There were few heroes and little sense of celebration.

When Springsteen charged onto the scene in the mid-'70s, his mission seemed to be to bring back the inspiration that rock had brought to his life.

"The greatest thing is going backstage after the show and seeing some kid there, not someone screwed up on drugs, but someone whose face is all lit up," he told me in 1978. "It's like you've done something to get things stirred up inside his head. That's the whole idea—get excited. . .do something. . .be your own hero."

But it took time for Springsteen to develop that rock-as-inspiration goal. He may have been born to run, but he wasn't born a leader. In the beginning, he was just like any other kid trying to find his way into this exciting world of rock & roll.

Springsteen went through a long evolutionary phase, much of it worked out in Asbury Park clubs. Bruce's parents moved to Northern California in 1969, but he stayed in New Jersey.

With the Earth band, Bruce became a local guitar hero at the Upstage, the area's main gathering spot for musicians. He attracted some of the area's best young musicians for his next band, Child, another Cream-accented outfit. The lineup included drummer Vini (Mad Dog) Lopez, who played on Springsteen's first two albums, and keyboardist Danny Federici, who is still part of the E Street Band. After changing its name to Steel Mill, the group built a considerable reputation on the East Coast. Southside Johnny Lyons, who was part of the Asbury Park scene at the time, looks back fondly on the excitement of those days: "We formed hundreds of bands for particular things we'd get interested in. . . I'd want to do something like Otis Redding or Muddy Waters, so I'd put together a band. Bruce would want to do Van Morrison or Dylan, so we'd try to find musicians who would play that stuff and an outlet to play it in.

"The best thing was the musical interaction. It was a situation where you'd be playing with someone you didn't know so you'd

Overleaf: Early E Street Beach Boys, from left: Clarence Clemons, Danny Frederici, Bruce, Vini Lopez, Garry Tallent, David Sancious.

have to react to the unknown quality. And it gave me a great insight into what can happen on stage: great things or terrible things. It made all of us more loose."

Bruce was a magnetic guitar hero. He led Steel Mill with bluesy Eric Clapton and Jimmy Page licks. Steel Mill fans still trade live tapes today, and many argue that this music was Bruce's finest hour. Their image of Bruce is a guy with long hair and patched jeans leaning into long improvisational guitar solos, not the working class hero of today.

In late 1969 Steel Mill traveled to California, where they played a few more shows and auditioned for Bill Graham's Fillmore record label. Tapes of the audition and of Steel Mill's performance at Berkeley's Matrix club that November reveal just how unfocused Springsteen was at the time. The Matrix performance featured seven- to ten-minute songs that combined the improvisation of jazz with the unyielding march of heavy-metal rock. Songs like "The War is Over" and "America Under Fire" were forceful, but contained few of the characteristics that would later be associated with Springsteen's work.

Steel Mill called it quits a few months after returning to New Jersey, but not before a significant personnel change. Steve Van Zandt replaced Vinny Roslyn on bass. Van Zandt deserves an introduction here because he would become not just a key member of the E Street Band, but Springsteen's closest friend.

Van Zandt grew up in Jersey not far from Asbury Park. He enjoyed early '60s hits like the Isley Brothers' "Twist and Shout" and Gene Chandler's "Duke of Earl," but he didn't begin thinking about becoming a musician until he saw the Rolling Stones on TV in the middle of that decade.

Van Zandt spent the next few years in and out of bands, chasing the same dream as Springsteen. But he eventually became disenchanted with rock's drift toward a more polished sound, and gave it up to work construction for a couple of years. He missed the music, though, and ended up joining the backup band for the Dovells, a group from the early '60s (known for the songs "Bristol Stomp" and "You Can't Sit Down") that worked the oldies' club circuit.

While in that band, Van Zandt started homing in on a musical direction, a fusion of rock and R&B that he would introduce with a band called the Asbury Jukes several years after the collapse of Steel Mill. He stayed with the Jukes until he rejoined Bruce and the E Street Band just before the release of *Born to Run* in 1975.

Van Zandt's guitar playing has always been strong, but the E Street band's melody lines have usually been led by the piano parts. Miami Steve's guitar stings along in the heavy mix and he has a secret technique. "I play everything at ten," he once said. "That's the great equalizer. You'd be surprised how similar everything sounds when you do that."

"I think Steve has more influence over Bruce than anyone else,"

"The best thing that ever happened to me was when I got thrown out of the first band I was in, and I went home and put on 'It's All Over Now' by the Rolling Stones and learned that guitar solo."

said Peter Philbin, who was Springsteen's closest contact at Columbia Records for years. "A lot of it is they were just thrown together early on. They had common experiences and common goals. They both wanted to be rockers. Steve supports Bruce very well, but at the same time wants to be his own man. That has gone back and forth for years.

"Whether in the band or out of it, they are so close emotionally that there is no separation. Steve innately knows how Bruce feels. He has a better sense than anyone, and that's important because Bruce doesn't talk about how he feels a lot. You either know it or you don't, and Steve is the best at knowing."

While organizing his next group after Steel Mill, Springsteen toyed around with a loose-knit collection of musicians called Dr. Zoom and the Sonic Boom that would probably have been forgotten long ago if it weren't for its zany name. But Bruce's attention was focused on another band: the Bruce Springsteen Band. Originally designed for ten pieces and a horn section, the group eventually dwindled to five, and it didn't last long even at that size. Times became tough in Asbury Park after a race riot during the summer of

Below: In the driver's seat, 1973, Asbury Park. Left: With David Sancious who took the solo route after the first two E Street albums. Overleaf: Bruce's parents left New Jersey for California, but he chose to stay and soak up the East Coast rays.

1971 devastated the boardwalk area. Springsteen would eventually be reunited with many of the musicians he worked with that year: Van Zandt, keyboardist David Sancious, saxophonist Clarence Clemons, bassist Garry Tallent. But after the Bruce Springsteen Band folded he tried it on his own for a while.

While the other musicians took day jobs to supplement their incomes, Springsteen continued to devote all his time to music. Trying every possible door, he auditioned for Mike Appel and Jim Cretecos, a minor level songwriting-production team whose major credit was writing one hit, "Don't You Want to Be Wanted," for teenybop faves the Partridge Family.

"I never got into being discouraged because I never got into hoping," Springsteen told me about this period. "When I was a kid, I never got used to expecting success. I got used to failing.

"Once you do that, the rest is real easy. It took a lot of the pressure off. I just said, 'Hell, I'm a loser. I don't have to worry about anything.' I assumed immediately that nothing was happening.

Southside Johnny Lyon (striped scarf) and the Asbury Jukes. Right, Bruce and Clarence, aka "The Big Man."

"But that's not the same as giving up. You keep trying, but you don't count on things. It can be a strength. Because I know some people who sweat out winning so much it kills them. So, in the end, they lose anyway. They win, but they lose. People don't realize things can often be just the opposite of what they seem."

Appel and Cretecos agreed to manage Springsteen early in 1972. The contract—signed at night on the hood of a car—would come to haunt Springsteen. At the time, however, Springsteen was busy writing songs "like a madman" as he has said often. "Had no money, nowhere to go, nothing to do. Didn't know too many people. It was cold and I wrote a lot. And I got to feeling very guilty if I didn't."

On May 3, Appel arranged for an audition with John Hammond, the CBS executive who had signed Bob Dylan a decade before. In *Born to Run*, Dave Marsh relates what happened when the cocky Appel first met Hammond. "You're the guy who discovered Bob Dylan, huh? Well, we want to find out if that was just luck or if you really have ears."

What a guy. It's not hard to see how Springsteen and Appel would clash eventually.

But that day in 1972, Springsteen nervously walked into the CBS office with Appel, sat at the piano and played almost a dozen songs, five of which showed up on his first album: "Growin' Up," "It's Hard to Be a Saint in the City," "Mary Queen of Arkansas," "Does This Bus Stop at 82nd Street?" and "The Angel." Hammond was excited by the imagination and dazzle of the words. Springsteen walked out of the room with a future.

•

I WAS OPEN TO THE PAIN AND CROSSED BY
    THE RAIN AND I WALKED ON A CROOKED
    CRUTCH
I STROLLED ALL ALONE THROUGH A
    FALLOUT ZONE AND CAME OUT WITH MY
    SOUL UNTOUCHED
I HID IN THE CLOUDED WRATH OF THE
    CROWN, BUT WHEN THEY SAID "SIT DOWN,"
    I STOOD UP—
OOOH...GROWIN' UP

•

As soon as the deal with Columbia Records was complete, Springsteen began gathering up the old gang—Clemons, Lopez, Tallent, Federici and Sancious—to make the record. The only trouble was that Hammond saw Springsteen as a folk-style singer-songwriter, not as a rock & roller. Like Mike Appel initially, Hammond didn't want anything to interfere with Springsteen's words.

The album, *Greetings from Asbury Park, N.J.*, was a compromise between Hammond's preference for folk and Springsteen's rock

Mike Appel, the man who moved moguls for Springsteen. He got the face-to-face interview with John Hammond of Columbia.

instincts. It was recorded in just three weeks and co-produced by Appel and Cretecos for Laurel Canyon Ltd., their publishing and production company.

Because of the folk emphasis, the LP seemed primarily a showcase for Springsteen's words. He was already dealing with the issues of integrity and responsibility that would be at the heart of his best work, but he hadn't developed much clarity as a writer. The influences of Dylan and Van Morrison ricochet through many of the songs, and some of the album's images are clumsy, even almost incomprehensible. Still, there was an enormous excitement and promise in the outpouring of images and rhymes, encompassing everything from Catholic school memories to Springsteen's relentless drive. The album overflowed with the sheer exhilaration of someone testing his creative prowess.

Springsteen's sound hadn't jelled yet either. His arrangements owed heavily to the soul and R&B stylings of Van Morrison, particularly the keyboard and horn sounds. The steady back beat suggests the famed Motown rhythm section, and the horn arrangements echo the Memphis Stax sound. It's big city music with smooth sax lines and handclaps over Bruce's miked acoustic guitar. He would almost talk his lyrics over David Sancious' spare, jazzy

Preceding page: Enter Miami Steve Van Zandt and Max Weinberg. Below: The first E Street band. Early on, the albums were playing characters and setting off each other.

piano and then build the tension with drums and guitars until the whole group joined in and rocked the song to its conclusion.

"I got a lot of things out in that first album," Springsteen told me in 1974. "I let out an incredible amount at once—a million things in each song. They were written in half-hour, fifteen-minute blasts. I don't know where they came from. A few of them I worked on for a week or so, but most of them were just jets, a real energy situation.

"I had all that stuff stored up for years, because there was no outlet in the bars I had been playing. No one's listening in a bar, and if they are, you've got a low PA system and they can't hear the words anyway. So that first album was a big outlet."

Years later, during the Born in the U.S.A. tour, he smiled when asked about the album. Sitting backstage at the Greensboro Coliseum, he said, "When I first started, I was pretty sure of myself. . . . I remember when I did my first record, I thought it was dynamite." He laughed at the memory of his early attitude. "I had a tremendous amount of confidence for some reason. Then I began to question my work extremely hard. I was no longer interested in what I was doing well, I was interested in what I was not doing well. I felt I was failing because part of the picture was missing. That began with the *Darkness* record and carried through to this one."

The first album, released in January 1973, was not a hit. First-year sales were only about 20,000, which wasn't enough to place the LP on *Billboard* magazine's weekly list of the nation's 200 top-selling records. But that didn't dampen Springsteen's spirits. He was making records and he had his band together again. Besides, critics were responding favorably to the album. In a widely circulated article in *Crawdaddy* magazine, Peter Knobler wrote with a passion that was typical of the early critical response:

"Two months ago, I was living under a sorry illusion. Jaded, sick to death of imitations and nostalgia and circular tangents, I figured rock & roll had priced itself out of its own salvation. Artists and Repertoire men were combing the coffeehouses and cellars of the country like major league scouts, offering bonus baby bribes to anyone within four octaves of the big-time.

"No one, my reasoning went, could possibly mature before being discovered and absolutely no one could do it afterwards. And because there were no transcendent phenoms coming out of the woodsheds, it looked like Bob Dylan and Babe Ruth were sadly safe.

"It turns out I was wrong.

"Bruce Springsteen has been hiding in New Jersey writing these incredible songs. He's 23, has spent the last eight or nine years playing in rock & roll bands, and sings with a freshness and urgency that I haven't heard since I was rocked by 'Like a Rolling Stone.'"

Like many other critics who discovered Springsteen at this time, Knobler pegged him as a "new Bob Dylan." But there was more to that response than critics looking for someone to fill a fallen hero's shoes. On his first record as on later ones, Springsteen created a personal response that required of reviewers something stronger than the usual critical prose. *Greetings from Asbury Park, N.J.* had caught many an influential ear, and though many were skeptical— remember, this was 1973—there were more who listened, with hope, for what Springsteen would do next.

"Everybody has it but most people just never figure it out," Springsteen once explained, talking about talent and potential. "You've got to be able to see yourself for what you are, and not until then can you be what you want to be."

In the weeks after the release of *Greetings from Asbury Park, N.J.* Springsteen was busy figuring out who he was. He was proud of the first album, but he knew that it was just a beginning—more an exercise in creative energy than a definition of his own vision.

His second album was released in November 1973, and went a long way toward codifying Springsteen's artistic identity. His first album may have had an Asbury Park postcard on its cover, but it was wildly jumbled in its locations and themes, as if his mind were so filled with images and emotions that he could hardly pin them down to a specific place. *The Wild, The Innocent and the E Street Shuffle* became his statement of roots.

The music celebrates a catalogue of American music styles: the churchy organ and carnival calliope sounds (reminiscent of Garth Hudson and Richard Manuel's keyboard interplay in the Band), the funky wah-wah over the lead guitar on "E Street Shuffle," the folk guitar and harmonica, the marching band tempos, the horns fat and mournful. Ariel Swartley picked this album as her desert island companion in Greil Marcus' anthology, *Stranded*, observing that Springsteen treats rock as "our common language, our shared mythology." We recognize the Spector echo, the James Brown funk sound and the "Dion-ysian brawls." Springsteen "triggers memories like you were a jukebox and he was the man with all the quarters." The band stretches out here, and their music is joyous, full of the soul choruses of the big ensemble groups that played Asbury Park's boardwalk roadhouses.

"I don't know what I'm writing from, but the main thing I've always been worried about was me," he explained. "I had to write about me all the time, every song, 'cause in a way, you're trying to find out what that 'me' is. That's why I chose where I grew up, and where I live, and I take situations I'm in, and people I know, and take them to the limits."

Sure there was good-time, Gary U.S. Bonds–style rock & roll— witness the frat-rock "everybody form a line" chants of "The E Street Shuffle." But despite those bursts of party-time energy, grimmer moods were starting to emerge in his music and lyrics. His songs told stories of people trapped by their environments: searching for love and transcendence in the streets of a Jersey shore town, over the river in the big city, or on the boardwalk on the Fourth of July. There were the sentimental strains of accordions and calliopes in his songs. Balancing that melancholia, though, was an increasing sense of seasoned, hard-won optimism: that the emptiness in people's lives could be overcome with compassion and a willingness to take risks.

Springsteen's philosophy was emerging. The vagabond circus image of "Wild Billy's Circus Story" was the perfect metaphor for

Springsteen's music draws from many American music sources: Motown, Stax-Volt, Dylan, Elvis and a little garage band music, too.

what rock & roll meant to him: membership in a lively but outcast community, and the rootlessness of the road. The life Springsteen saw ahead was exciting, certainly, but also hard, often lonely. Springsteen wasn't thinking of rock & roll as a path to luxury. He was thinking truths.

The album included two songs which would become audience favorites for years to come. "Rosalita (Come out Tonight)" was a typically autobiographical effort: a witty, libidinous tale of a rock star and his girlfriend that became Bruce's best-loved song. Its sassy digressions and fun-loving knocks at parental disapproval showed Bruce assuming control over his story-telling, beginning to marshal his powers of observation into coherent, pungent frameworks.

"4th of July, Asbury Park (Sandy)" showed a more wistful side, the verses whispered as if he was singing into his girlfriend's ear. This was a Springsteen ready to acknowledge failure ("Sandy, that waitress I was seeing lost her desire for me/I spoke with her last night, she said she won't set herself on fire for me anymore"), a Springsteen looking for love but looking even more for a way out of his dead-end existence. More than "Rosalita," "4th of July" had an intimacy and an immediacy that was deeply affecting.

I had enjoyed Springsteen's first two albums, even putting the second on the 1974 year-end Ten Best list I compiled for the Los Angeles *Times*. So when I saw that he was coming through town that summer, opening for Dr. John, I called Columbia Records and asked for an interview. To my surprise, the publicist called back to say Springsteen wasn't doing any interviews. Everyone in rock & roll does interviews—except Dylan. Was this guy starting to take that "New Dylan" stuff seriously?

I didn't press the matter. Life goes on and, besides, Arista Records had been nagging me to do a profile of its new president, Clive Davis, the Sunday I was planning to write about Springsteen.

I mentioned the Davis interview to the Columbia publicist and got a surprising response. Columbia was having its national convention in Los Angeles the Sunday the Davis story would appear, and since Davis—the man who had okayed John Hammond's recommendation to sign Springsteen—had recently been ousted as president of CBS Records, the last thing the local CBS office wanted was a big spread on Davis, possibly quoting him about how much more he enjoyed life now that he was away from CBS.

After talking to her bosses at CBS, the publicist called back to ask if there wasn't some way I could run the Davis interview some other Sunday. I said sure: I'd postpone Davis a week if I could get Springsteen. The word was relayed that afternoon from CBS: deal.

I don't know what CBS did to get Bruce to do the interview, but I later learned that label executives in New York had to step in and convince Springsteen to talk. As I headed for the Santa Monica Civic Auditorium that night, I wondered what this guy Springsteen was like. Who ever would have expected the guy who wrote songs as marvelous as "Sandy" and "Rosalita" to be a prima donna?

Playing from memory: "There ain't a note I play onstage that can't be traced directly back to my mother and father."

I had asked for the interview to be after the show so that I could see Springsteen perform first. By the time he stepped off the stage, I was no longer concerned with Bruce's manner. I just wanted to learn more about him. The show wasn't nearly as focused as it would become, and it was only forty-five minutes compared to the eventual norm of three hours. But it was amazing.

Wearing a white undershirt, black pants and dark shades, Springsteen hit the stage looking like the epitome of white-boy punk. He didn't play the pouty sex-symbol games of a Mick Jagger, nor the standoffish unpredictability of a Bob Dylan. From the first number, Springsteen practically attacked the microphone with his voice, roaring his songs into it with bar band energy yet with a greater sense of significance and even grandeur. Grabbing an electric guitar, he snaked across the stage—to the shrieks of male and female fans alike. Yet the move didn't seem calculated. Like the whole show, it was a spontaneous, unpretentious example of the incensing power of rock & roll to move an audience.

Springsteen's mission wasn't clear at this point, but he was obviously aiming for high stakes. Separating himself from the recycled steps of most rock contenders, he was trying to establish a new and lasting relationship with his audience. For most of the show, he and the E Street Band gave the audience up-tempo tunes, songs bristling with the fire, energy and passion of the old Asbury Park clubs. For the encore, however, he played the slow, disarming "New York Serenade," a tune that distracted from the strong energy level that had been building. The applause was less when he finished than if he had done something more lively.

"I thought it was important to do that song," he said backstage. "It completes the set for me. It might get more response to do a boom-boom thing and really rock the joint. But when I walked down the steps afterwards I felt complete. Otherwise, I feel messed up.

1975: Jon Landau, Springsteen and girlfriend Karen Darbin.

"It's just being honest with the audience and with myself, I guess. You can't conform to the formula of always giving the audience what it wants or you're killing yourself and you're killing the audience.

"Just because they respond to something doesn't mean they want it. I think it has come to the point where they respond automatically to things they think they should respond to. You've got to give them more than that. Someone has to take the initiative and say, 'Let's step out of the mold. Let's try this.'"

There was lots of kidding backstage, but there wasn't the hedonistic edge associated with the backstage scene at most rock concerts. Bruce wasn't into drugs or groupies. He also wasn't into publicity. He shook hands, but certainly didn't give the impression he was overjoyed about being interviewed.

After a half hour watching Dr. John's set, he led me across the street to the hotel. Springsteen seemed uncomfortable as he sat on the bed, rubbing his hand through his short, stubbly beard. I couldn't tell if he was shy or just didn't like to be asked questions. He asked why I wanted to talk to him and whether it wasn't better to let fans just listen to the music rather than read about the artist as well.

Even today, Bruce is not big on interviews, though he does agree to a few after the release of most of his albums because he feels some communication with his audience beyond the songs is appropriate. But he tries to keep most of the interviews to relatively short encounters backstage after shows.

The irony is if a fan or the same writer bumps into him on the street when he's got some free time, Bruce'll sit and talk for hours. The reason for this contrast is that Bruce has always been suspicious of the celebration of the individual. He worries that it'll distract both him and his audience from the really important thing about him: the music.

It was apparent quite early in the interview that Springsteen was different from most of the rock stars I had met. I was used to image-conscious performers who had pat answers to most questions and worked hard at convincing you they were larger than life. They also tended to entertain or flatter you in hopes of securing a favorable write-up.

Bruce was simply himself or—in the word that his fans would often use to describe him over the years—he was "real." There was no edge or self-consciousness about him as he searched in a sometimes halting manner for answers to my questions. It was hard to believe that this was the same dynamic guy I had seen on stage.

Talking about the songs he was writing then—which would end up on *Born to Run*—his seriousness impressed me. "The writing is more difficult now. On this album, I started slowly to find out who I am and where I wanted to be. It was like coming out of the shadow of various influences and trying to be me. You have to let out more of yourself all the time. You strip off the first layer, then the second, then the third. It gets harder because it's more personal." More than anyone I had ever interviewed, I could see that Springsteen wasn't just aiming for success. He was aiming for *truth.*

The word sounds corny now, but there was something about Springsteen that made it seem reasonable in person. Here was someone who was onto something new. I didn't know quite what it was, but I found myself pulling for him. I had loved rock ever since the first time I saw Elvis, too, but I wasn't sure I put quite as much faith in it as Springsteen did. Rock had lost a lot of its heart in the '70s. Could he make us all believe in it again?

The Wild, the Innocent still didn't establish Springsteen as a commercial force. It, too, failed to crack the *Billboard* Top 200 list, selling only about 50,000 copies in its first year. But the LP earned Springsteen even more critical support than *Greetings*. That support may have kept Springsteen on Columbia Records, where he was on delicate ground after Clive Davis was fired in 1973.

A cadre of Springsteen supporters at Columbia continued to believe in him and they saw the glowing reviews as a sign that he could break through commercially if he just got more exposure. Radio airplay, except in a few East Coast areas, had been almost nonexistent on the first two albums.

The most important review in Columbia's eyes appeared in the May 22 issue of Boston's *Real Paper.* It was written by Jon Landau, one of the half-dozen most important critics in the country. Besides writing for the *Real Paper,* he edited the *Rolling Stone* record review section.

"It's four in the morning and raining. I'm 27 today, feeling old, listening to my records, and remembering that things were different a decade ago. In 1964, I was a freshman at Brandeis University, playing guitar and banjo five hours a day, listening to records most of the rest of the time, jamming with friends during the late-night hours, working out the harmonies to Beach Boys' and Beatles' songs."

Describing a loss of enthusiasm he had felt as he became more involved with the music business as a record producer and critic, Landau continued.

"Today I listen to music with a certain measure of detachment. I'm a professional and I make my living commenting on it. There are months when I love my work and months when I hate it, going through the routine just as a shoe salesman goes through his.

"But tonight there is someone I can write of the way I used to write, without reservations of any kind. Last Thursday, at the Harvard Square theater, I saw my rock 'n' roll past flash before my eyes. And I saw something else: I saw rock 'n' roll future and its name is Bruce Springsteen. And on a night when I needed to feel young, he made me feel like I was hearing music for the very first time."

Columbia Records made "rock 'n' roll future" the cornerstone of a massive campaign.

Springsteen was on such shaky ground at CBS in the months after *The Wild, the Innocent* that the label asked him to do what amounts to a test recording before they allowed him to proceed with the third album. He went into the studio and cut the song "Born to Run." In retrospect it's easy to think that anyone could see that "Born to Run" was a classic rock & roll track. But no one cheered as Bruce walked out of the studio. This rendition of "Born to Run" was

Springsteen and the old E Street band bed down in Cambridge, Mass., 1973 with Joe Spadafora (white socks), the owner of Joe's Place.

muddy, heightening suspicions around the company that Springsteen just couldn't make a commercial record. The track also cost $10,000, considered an outrageous amount at the time. Alarmed executives wondered what the whole album would cost.

Besides, CBS thought Bruce had an attitude problem. The label had worked hard on a plan to get Springsteen exposure. They helped him get the opening slot on a national tour by Chicago, one of Columbia's biggest acts. But Bruce quit the tour after only about a dozen shows. He felt he couldn't capture all the emotional aspects of his music in the thirty or forty-five minutes that was allotted to him as an opening act. He declared that in the future he would appear only as a headliner.

The reaction at CBS was that he must be crazy. He took too much time between records, his lyrics were too long, his vocals were hard to understand, he wouldn't show up at radio stations for promotions, and he didn't even want to do interviews.

Bruce just didn't think any of that was his concern. His business was music. It was Mike Appel's job to stand between Bruce and the company. And the abrasive way Appel passed that message to Columbia was another mark against Springsteen.

But the reviews helped and so did the enthusiasm of people like publicists Ron Oberman and Peter Philbin and promotion director Mike Pillot. Springsteen and Appel went back into the studio and remixed "Born to Run."

During the months before the release of *Born to Run*, Springsteen became involved in a growing partnership with Jon Landau. The critic moved to New York, for reasons that had nothing to do with Springsteen, and began attending some of the *Born to Run* album sessions. Springsteen had been bogged down in the project. He was having trouble getting the wide-screen sounds in his head onto record. Landau offered helpful perspective. By March 1975, Landau was officially listed as co-producer.

According to everyone involved, the sessions were grueling. Springsteen knew he was onto a breakthrough and he refused to compromise.

"I was unsure about the album all the way," he explained shortly after it was released. "I didn't really know what I put down on it. I lost all perspective...the [sessions] turned into something I never conceived of a record turning into. It turned into this thing that was wrecking me, just pounding me into the ground. Every time you'd win a little victory over it, accomplish a little something you'd say, 'Well, the worst is over.' The next day you'd come back in and it would start pounding away at you again."

Landau, coming into the project fresh, helped Springsteen edit some songs and tighten arrangements. Of Springsteen's tireless insistence on looking at every song from every angle, someone close to Springsteen once said, "The indecision comes from fear. If you do one thing, that means you can't do another. Bruce wants it all. He always wants it all."

All business: Springsteen, Clemons and Frederici.

**4**. *Born to Run* breathed with the same kind of discovery that made Elvis Presley's *Sun Sessions* and Bob Dylan's *Highway 61 Revisited* the two most important American rock albums before it. Listening to all three works, you feel present at the forging of a major artistic vision. You sense the artist's excitement at finding something within himself that he hadn't known was there until it burst forth in the studio.

While *Sun Sessions*, Presley's first recordings, unveiled rock & roll as we now define it, and *Highway 61 Revisited* updated the energy and drive of early rock and added a fierce intelligence, *Born to Run* demonstrated that Springsteen had the instincts, ambition and knowledge of rock's history to put the pieces of the fragmented rock scene back together. It was the purest glimpse in nearly a decade of the passion and power that had once been rock's hallmarks.

First there was "Thunder Road." An earlier generation had seen the elements of their romantic dreams symbolized by Fred Astaire and Ginger Rogers in the "Night and Day" sequence of *The Gay Divorcee*: an elegant ballroom, two glasses of champagne and a cheek-to-cheek dance. "Thunder Road" defined and celebrated a different dream of romance for a new generation: a car, a stretch of road and "one last chance to make it real."

Early demos reveal that while the song's pining, urgent melody took shape over time, its stunning lyrics were there from the beginning. Springsteen's images in "Thunder Road" are as immediate as Chuck Berry's and as haunting as Dylan's: Mary dancing alone on the porch, in her bed yearning for her lost loves, her boyfriends crying out her name into the nighttime air. It's a sad portrait that's redeemed by one last hope: "Tonight we will be free/All the promises will be broken," he cries, climaxing this tale of passionate love and personal transcendence that moves me as much today as it did when I first heard it.

But lyrics were only one part of Springsteen's design. Springsteen was as concerned with the sound of the record. The music was fiery, sensual and intense. Springsteen was nowhere near the pure singer Presley was, but he is arrestingly effective in the gritty, vernacular manner of Dylan.

The music itself is best represented by the album's title track, as triumphant a synthesis as we're likely to hear of everything that has been important in American rock & roll. What Phil Spector did for maximum sound at one take with wall of sound hits like "Then He Kissed Me," "Uptown" and "Baby I Love You," is what Springsteen, Appel and Landau produced—in their own version—for the '70s. If the drums, cymbals, piano and organ don't cover the audio spectrum, the guitars, voices and saxes surely will. *Born to Run* is lush. It's one big meal of a record. Vini Lopez and David Sancious had left the band, and their drum and piano spots were taken by Max Weinberg and Roy Bittan respectively. Weinberg played drums like his idols Levon Helm of the Band (Max even covers his snare with heavy paper towels to get that flat, wooden Memphis blues drum sound) and Ringo Starr, the king of the immovable, rock solid backbeat. Bittan's piano playing is strong and versatile. He is com-

fortable in many styles and serves as the transitional player during the live shows. Danny Federici's organ swirls in the mix and he wields his famed electric glockenspiel with inspired abandon. Its romantic, evocatory chiming coupled with Springsteen and Van Zandt's majestic guitar lines make "Born to Run" sound like Roy Orbison leading the world's funkiest halftime marching band.

Springsteen sings much more effectively on "Born to Run," and he's never sounded more confident. He shouts, growls and catches his voice like Elvis and Orbison did when they sang on the Sun label. Clarence solos like King Curtis, Bittan is funky, and bassist Gary Tallent and Weinberg click immediately. Springsteen stitched these elements together with an urgent, anthemic edge that made the record seem the work of an obsessed artist who feared he might never get another chance in the studio—or the passion of someone touched by a vision.

Make no mistake: *Born to Run* wasn't a flawless album. Just as Springsteen leaned too heavily on influences like Dylan, Van Morrison and the Band in his first album, the sources of some of the ideas on "Born to Run" lie too near the surface, from the Phil Spector-style orchestration of many of the songs to the Dylanesque organ introduction to "Backstreets." Still, the album's best selections are revelations of the highest order in rock.

Springsteen has often said that he felt reborn the night he wrote "Born to Run," and his thrill and confidence spilled over to the E Street Band's recording of the cut and the live shows.

It's no accident that the members of the band nicknamed Springsteen "the Boss." He doesn't dominate absolutely—there is room for group members to express themselves—but his word is final, though all band shares of the concert take are equal (to new guy Nils Lofgren's amazement). Bruce will get incensed if an E Streeter misses a song cue. When he brings his arm down, Max Weinberg hits the drum. What he wants on the record goes on the record. Bruce doesn't have to threaten, but he has his rules: no drugs, be on time, be on the bus when it leaves. Though the band's personnel was stable from the time of *Born to Run* up to the Born in the U.S.A. tour, there were some changes required earlier. Vini Lopez, the drummer, occasionally would speed up the beat on stage, and, according to a longtime associate of Springsteen's, Bruce was probably not too disappointed when Lopez left the band. Ernest "Boom" Carter replaced him. David Sancious is an outstanding pianist and Bruce admired his technical ability. But Sancious and Springsteen's musical ideas began to diverge. Perhaps, the associate has noted, his long, fluid solos seemed out of place in the band's arrangements. David's parting with the E Street Band was amicable and he left to make his own albums, taking Lopez's replacement, Carter, with him.

Preceding page: Bruce and Miami Steve play The Carlton Theater in Red Bank, New Jersey, October, 1975. Left, After a grueling summer in the studio making *Born to Run*, Springsteen had every reason to sound exultant in concert. "Born to Run" was a hit single (at four and a half minutes long) and this was his first national tour.

The *Born to Run* lineup:

Clarence Clemons' hard-blowing sax work and playful stage presence have made him the best-known member of the E Street Band. Nicknamed "Big Man" (though on the back of *The Wild, The Innocent and the E Street Shuffle* his nickname is "Nick"). Clemons was born in 1942 in Virginia, and played minor league football until an auto accident ended his career. Large in form but soft-spoken and gentle offstage, Clemons worked as a counselor in a reform school, blowing sax on the weekends. By the early '70s, Clemons was bored with soul outfits and hooked up with an Asbury Park band that specialized in rock oldies. That's where Springsteen spotted him. Though some saxophonists see Clemons as a one-dimensional player—ace session man Ernie Watts savagely parodied Clemons' style on Randy Newman's "My Life Is Good"—his persona, especially as a foil to Springsteen, is a crucial element to the band's onstage chemistry.

Roy Bittan, dubbed "the Professor" by Springsteen because he studied music at Brooklyn College, was born on New York's Long Island in 1949. He had done keyboard work for various outfits and had played for some traveling musicals when he spotted Springsteen's ad in the *Village Voice* and made what he calls "the quickest phone call of my life." Urbane and easy-going, Bittan was to become one of the most influential rock & roll pianists of the period, thanks in large measure to his work on the longer pieces on *Born to Run*: "Backstreets" and "Jungleland."

Danny Federici, known as "Phantom" because of his more unassuming qualities, was nineteen when he first met Springsteen in 1969 at the Upstage in Asbury Park. About his days with Bruce in Steel Mill, Federici recalled, "At this point Bruce was writing a song a day. It was crazy. It got so I was dreading going to rehearsals, knowing that there was going to be a new bunch of songs to be learned every time. And all that material is gone now. Bruce is the kind of guy who just says, 'Oh—that was yesterday,' and throws it all away." Though not as accomplished a player as Bittan, it was Federici who plunked out the glockenspiel-settings that flavored so much of Bruce's work during this period.

Bassist Garry Tallent, one of the most avid collectors of vintage rock and rockabilly 45's alive, also met Bruce in 1969 in Asbury Park, where he'd moved from his native Detroit. Once the band's most hirsute member, Tallent's rugged good looks now resemble Sam Shepard's.

"No Jr. Ginger Bakers, please" read the ad that drummer Max Weinberg responded to and that resulted in his being made a member of the E Street Band. Born in South Orange in 1951, "Mighty Max" initially sought to be a guitarist, but switched to drums because that was the only instrument available when he started taking music in school. Cordial and witty offstage, Weinberg enjoys showmanship in all its forms (he's a big Liberace fan) and is a student of drumming (to this day, he's mad at himself for slowing down during "Bad-

Right: Clarence Clemons. Following pages: Danny Federici, Garry Tallent, Miami Steve Van Zandt, Roy Bittan, Max Weinberg.

lands"). Weinberg's *The Big Beat*, a collection of lively interviews with his favorite rock drummers, was published in 1984.

Guitarist "Miami" Steve Van Zandt, never seen with a bare head, filled out the roster. With him in the band, Springsteen no longer had to cover every guitar lead and could concentrate on performing and singing. Van Zandt's turn-in-up-to-ten style and gutbucket backup vocals lent the band the extra punch it needed.

As for Bruce's guitar playing, both on record and in concert it was becoming much more economical; Bruce was editing his marathon solos from Steel Mill days into lean soulful four-bar fills.

The new unit jelled quickly and the Born to Run shows were hailed in city after city as among the finest ever in rock. Springsteen had shed the dark glasses and become more accessible on stage. One thing that made Springsteen so appealing live was the fullness of his sound. The saxophone and two keyboards provided more punctuation and flavoring than most bands offered in the '70s. Also Bruce conveyed an irresistible degree of energy. He stepped away from the cold, impersonal stance of so many rockers to weave intriguing narratives—some playful, some poignant—into the show.

Mostly, he took chances, giving each show a feeling of uniqueness. He'd even surprise the band by suddenly reprising an old Beatles or Presley tune, or reaching back for one of the seldom played tunes from his first album. After all the elaborate production of the *Born to Run* album, he'd open shows on the 1975 tour with an acoustic version of "Thunder Road"—just him on stage, backed by a piano.

Rather than do the song in the spirited style of the record, he sang it in a gentle, melancholy way. Though the more upbeat version would have been a safer opening for the show, Springsteen gave the audience something to remember.

On October 2, 1975, three weeks before the *Time* and *Newsweek* covers, Springsteen sat out a bomb scare at Milwaukee's Uptown Theater by knocking back a few drinks at his hotel's bar. As the usual teetotaler put it, he "got a little loose" and later turned in a thumping, crazed performance at the midnight show. Earlier, on the way back to the Uptown, Springsteen got on top of a British writer's car, causing the driver to comment, "I have seen the future of rock & roll and he is on my windshield."

Where most rock shows seem so programmed that you get the feeling you could walk into the show at 9:30 P.M. on consecutive nights and hear the identical guitar lick, Bruce made each show breathe with the excitement of knowing no other show would be exactly like it. He might drop in a new song that he wouldn't do again for a year, or he might reinterpret an old song. Either way, this upstart from New Jersey was setting the rock world on its ear. Cynics were claiming it was all hype, but audiences were spreading a different word.

So were the critics.

In a *Rolling Stone* review, Dave Marsh compared Springsteen to greats, including Dylan and Pete Townshend. In the *Village Voice*, Paul Nelson wrote, "Springsteen fashions the kind of seamless, 150-minute performance that most artists only dream about."

The continuous press support was accompanied this time by considerable radio airplay. Along with the audience that Springsteen had captured with his live shows, the exposure was enough to push the album into the Top 10 within weeks of its September 1 release. The first two albums—which had crept onto the sales charts in July—eventually made it up to the Top 75. The issues of *Time* and *Newsweek* that featured Springsteen on their covers were published the week of October 27.

Joe Smith, then president of Warner Brothers Records, pointed to the success of *Born to Run* as the first time reviewers had created a star by themselves. "There have been critical favorites in the past, but it was never as unanimous as it was with Springsteen," Smith said. "They eventually convinced enough people to give him a try."

Springsteen was definitely rolling. In view of all the hoopla, a backlash was inevitable. The most widely circulated of the anti-Springsteen articles appeared October 5 in the New York *Times*. Henry Edwards, a freelance contributor, came up with a line that was almost as quoted at the time as Landau's "future of rock." Edwards wrote, "If there hadn't been a Bruce Springsteen, then the Critics Would Have Made Him Up."

Edwards' argument was that Springsteen was a mediocre talent who had been hyped into stardom by Columbia Records and nostalgia-minded critics. "Springsteen's raw dynamics, for all the fun they may provide, simply cannot disguise the fact that for the most part Springsteen's lyrics are an effusive jumble, his melodies either second-handed or undistinguished and his performance tedious."

Springsteen went on to record four of the greatest rock albums ever made. Edwards went on to write the screenplay for the film *Sgt. Pepper's Lonely Hearts Club Band*.

Much of the industry debate after the *Time* and *Newsweek* covers wasn't as much over Springsteen's artistry as whether the massive media attention would hurt or help him. Amid this whirlwind, one person, Mike Appel, wasn't the least worried. For the ex-Marine from Brooklyn, the covers were part of an optimistic master plan.

"There's something magical about those covers to me," Appel told me the morning the magazines hit the stands. "It goes back to 1956 when I was sitting in a doctor's office thumbing through a magazine.

"I don't remember if it was *Look* or *Life*, but there was a picture of a guy with all these girls reaching out for him. I wondered who he was and why the girls were after him. That was my introduction to Elvis Presley.

"The same thing happened with the Beatles in '64. I was looking at a magazine in a bus station when I saw a picture of these four guys. I hadn't heard their music yet, either, but I was fascinated. I made sure I checked them out, too.

"If I had a weak artist, I'd be a nervous wreck because of all the attention. But I've got Bruce Springsteen. That's why I know the *Time* and *Newsweek* covers will be to our advantage."

In fact, the *Time* and *Newsweek* covers were simply the most visible pieces in an extraordinary amount of critical support for Springsteen that dated back to the first album. It was the news and feature space devoted to Springsteen—rather than the amount of advertising space purchased by Columbia Records—that led to the charges that Springsteen was a hype.

The Columbia promotion budget for *Born to Run*, estimated at between $100,000 and $150,000, was hefty for an unproven seller, but the ads were dwarfed by the amount of space publications allocated to news and feature stories about Springsteen and the album. Everyone from Appel to the publicity staff at Columbia agrees that the *Time* and *Newsweek* covers were not only unsolicited, but more than anyone expected at the time.

When *Newsweek* contacted Columbia about doing a story for its music section on Springsteen, an interview was requested. To Columbia's chagrin, Appel said no. The only way Springsteen would do an interview was for a cover story. (Appel was so insistent on the "no cover, no interview" rule that Columbia publicists had to spend several hours convincing him that *Playboy*, which had requested an interview, only put bunnies on its covers.)

When *Newsweek* went ahead with a short article anyway, Appel figured the magazine wouldn't consider another Springsteen article for months. So he was startled when *Newsweek* called back a few weeks later, holding out the possibility of a cover for an interview. He was even more surprised when *Time* called a few days later with a similar offer.

"Hollywood couldn't have manufactured a better story," Appel said. "If there was any hyping, it was the press hyping itself. All I did was coordinate it. They came to us."

Despite Appel's optimism, the exposure was dangerous for Springsteen. Not only did the exposure set up difficult-to-meet

Bette Midler, a not-so-muscle-bound Bruce and D.J. Ed Sciaky 1975.

75 CENTS
OCTOBER 27, 1975
TIME®
Rock's New Sensation
Bruce Springsteen

expectations, it caused a backlash among those who feel the need to resist anything that's sold too hard. Discovery is part of the rock experience, and all the press attention had taken that possibility away from the fans.

Springsteen wasn't enthralled with the idea of the covers. Appel had to browbeat him into doing the interviews, inviting the *Time* reporter, for instance, on an airplane flight with them and then making sure that the reporter was seated next to Bruce. Even when the magazines came out, Springsteen tried to ignore them. But Steve Van Zandt bought dozens of copies of each and plastered them all over Bruce's room.

It would have been safer for Springsteen to have his career progress gradually but steadily from the first album through the Top 10 success of *Born to Run*. But pop artists cannot choose their own ground rules or conditions. The fact is Springsteen's career did not progress steadily. His first two records received virtually no airplay and he couldn't get concert bookings in most parts of the country. Even with all the attention and sales, *Born to Run* still wasn't being played on many major Top 40 stations.

The future might have been tougher for Springsteen because of the way he had come to the public's attention, but there might not have been a future without all the exposure. Springsteen finally had an audience. His future would depend on how well he reacted to the pressures and challenges. The important thing, in the end, would be the appeal of his music.

Ultimately, Appel was right. Springsteen was good enough to withstand the obstacles. Only Appel wasn't there to enjoy the victory.

"I haven't changed, but things around me have changed," Springsteen told me a week before the covers hit the stands. "I'm not sure what it all means yet. I haven't had time to sit down and decide what's new that's fun and what's new that's not.

"But I do wonder about it sometimes. What am I doing on the cover of *Time* and *Newsweek*? I'm not the president. I'm really just a simple guy. I got my band and my music, and I love 'em both. That's my world. My life. It always has been."

This was the first time I had seen Bruce since the Santa Monica show a year before. I had gone to his afternoon soundcheck at the Roxy in West Hollywood and was now riding back to the hotel with him and Glen Brunman, a Columbia publicist and another of the long-time supporters of Springsteen in the company.

As the car moved down Sunset Blvd., Brunman pointed out a huge *Born to Run* billboard on top of a building. I turned around and looked at it through the car's back window. Doing so, I could see Springsteen tensed in the backseat and his house-size photo on the billboard through the window. Brunman slowed down so that he, too, could see the billboard. The only person who wasn't looking was Springsteen.

Most rock stars would be thrilled at the sudden upswing in their

The hype rained down on the newsstands and the billboards, but the music was still the thing that would make or break Springsteen.

career, but Springsteen was already anxious about the changes in his life. He seemed trapped, off-stride.

Some quotes seem far more interesting in retrospect. Bruce's remarks actually defined his whole purpose. But they seemed so matter of fact at the time that I buried them in the story I wrote the next day.

Asked if all that was being written about him put added pressure on him when he went on stage, Springsteen replied, "I don't know if it makes it any harder. It has always been hard in a way. Everytime you get on stage, you have to prove something. It doesn't matter if they've heard you or not. The kid on the street will make up his own mind. The music is what really matters. That's the way it has always been."

As Brunman turned off Sunset toward the hotel, Springsteen heard the faint sounds of the Byrds' version of Dylan's "My Back Pages" on the car radio. "Turn it up," he shouted. "Turn it up." The car was already at the hotel, but Bruce didn't get out. He leaned back against the seat, closing his eyes as he listened. It was his first chance to relax in a hectic day of sound checks and photo sessions. The way he slumped against the seat told more about the hectic pace and demands made upon him than he would say.

Springsteen seemed totally refreshed, however, by the time he stepped on stage that night at the Roxy. There were slow spots in Springsteen's show; the occasional miniscenes, in which he tried to recapture the feel of a New Jersey street as an introduction to a song, weren't as natural or as affecting as they would become later.

There were also uneven moments musically. Because the *Born to Run* album was such a major advance in Springsteen's writing, the older songs—including "Spirit in the Night" and "The E Street Shuffle"—seemed to drag in comparison. In light of all the media attention, it was important to remember that Springsteen was still a growing artist.

But Springsteen was as stirring in his best moments on stage as anyone in rock. The magic of his show was that it combined entertainment and purpose. He could delight you with his antics—including dancing on the table tops—but he could also touch you deeply with songs as gloriously affirming as any in rock.

These songs from *Born to Run* told us where Springsteen was coming from and where he wanted to go. To continue growing artistically, he would have to begin examining the consequences of that journey.

Looking back on that period, Springsteen said at the start of the Born in the U.S.A. tour, "[That album] really dealt with faith and a searching for answers... I laid out a set of values. A set of ideas...intangibles like faith and hope, belief in friendship and in a better way.

"But you don't really know what those values are worth until you test them. So many things happened to me so fast... I always felt that if the music was right, I would survive. But if that went wrong, then that was the end of it."

Bruce patrolling the outfield during an E Street softball game. Baserunners respected his songwriting, but what about his arm?

The Born to Run tour should have been among the happiest days of Springsteen's life, but they turned into some of the worst. Long sensitive to the destructive side effects of fame, he began wondering if he, too, wasn't becoming overwhelmed. Suddenly he was a dollar sign to lots of people and that brought complications—or as he prefers to say, distractions.

"There was all the publicity and all the backlash," he told me in 1980. "I felt the thing I wanted most in life—my music—being swept away and I didn't know if I could do anything about it.

"That bothered me a lot, being perceived as an invention, a ship passing by. I'd been playing for ten years. I knew where I came from, every inch of the way. I knew what I believed and what I wanted."

After a brief U.S. tour, Springsteen and the E Street band flew to Europe in November 1975 for a few promotional dates, including two nights at the Hammersmith Odeon in London, where Springsteen was beginning to attract some attention but was still far from a bestseller. CBS's London staff, eager to duplicate what it saw as the spirit of Columbia's U.S. campaign, pounded the promotional drums. Stickers were plastered all over town and the Odeon walls declaring, AT LAST LONDON IS READY FOR BRUCE SPRINGSTEEN.

Springsteen, sensitive to charges of hype back home, went into an uncharacteristic rage when he saw the posters. He raced around the theater, ripping them down, and—according to a report in *Melody Maker*—even considered canceling the show. On stage, he was subdued.

About that night, he later recalled, "I felt I was in my 'I Walked With a Zombie' routine. It was nothin' to do with the place. It was me. It was the inside world. It's a hard thing to explain, but I learned a lot about my strengths and weaknesses in those days, especially on that particular night."

Mike Appel recognized the severity of the problem. "Bruce was so mad that night in London," he explained. "He went really nuts. And I guess I looked just as guilty to him as CBS. He lumped me in with *Time* and *Newsweek*. He wanted that fame and glory, but I guess he wanted it on his own terms."

The learning process wasn't over. After a couple months off, Springsteen resumed touring in the U.S.—and his spirits were even lower. The night of February 15, 1977, in Detroit was the first time in his life that he didn't want to go on stage.

"At that moment, I could see how people get into drinking or into drugs, because the one thing you want at a time like that is to be distracted—in a big way," he told me.

To understand Springsteen's despair at this point, you have to look at what originally attracted him to rock. Bruce has said over and over that rock & roll brought purpose to his life. He felt good about himself for the first time when he started playing the guitar. He also discovered that the more he devoted himself to his music, the better he felt. He saw the music as a test of his will and integrity and saw that his future was tied to it. His pursuit of that future bordered on an obsession.

Bruce had gone from a fairly happy guy who was selling 50,000 albums to selling 1.2 million, and he found his world being turned upside down. The fame was threatening the music.

The backlash and upheaval, however, weren't the only things bothering Springsteen. His management contract with Appel had only one more year to run, and Appel was pressuring him to renew it. Rather than draft a new contract, Springsteen preferred a less formal, oral arrangement.

Appel kept pushing for a written deal. Trying to convince Springsteen, he pointed out how much better the new contract would be than the old one. The strategy backfired, because it made Springsteen realize how bad the old deal was.

According to published reports, the contract with Laurel Canyon gave Bruce only a 3 percent royalty rate on the wholesale price (about ten cents), while Laurel Canyon received 10 percent (about forty cents). Instead of the usual 15 to 20 percent management commission, Laurel Canyon received 50 percent. In addition, Appel's company controlled all of Bruce's publishing. This may have been the sorest point of all.

Springsteen, for instance, couldn't even give Dave Marsh permission to use lines from his songs in Marsh's book *Born to Run* without Appel's permission. Wealth was never important to Springsteen, but his songs meant everything.

Before the 1976 tour, Springsteen spoke to an attorney who stressed the unfairness of the contract. Springsteen apparently still wanted to work things out. Appel had once mortgaged his house to keep Bruce and the band afloat. But things fell apart just before the Detroit shows.

"People would always say, 'Gee, it must have been tough for you.' But I always remember being in a good mood, being happy even through the bad stuff and the disappointments, because I knew I was ahead of nine out of ten other people that I've seen around me...because I was doing something that I liked."

As the dispute with Appel dragged on, Springsteen decided to begin work on the next album. He booked studio time and asked Jon Landau to produce the LP. Appel blocked the plans, invoking terms of the Laurel Canyon contract which gave the company the right to name Springsteen's producer.

Shortly afterward, Springsteen sued Appel in federal court in New York, charging fraud, breach of trust and undue influence. Appel quickly obtained an injunction barring Springsteen from recording with Landau. Rather than switch producers, Springsteen simply shelved the album until the legal tussle with Appel was resolved.

Looking back, Appel said in 1978, "What they offered me after three and a half years was less than adequate, and their lawyer made it impossible to make a deal. I think Springsteen needed an education. Contracts can be amended. They don't have to be broken off. But I was the central figure in his life, and I'm not the kind of guy who backs down."

Springsteen has avoided discussing the topic. But he did say early during the Darkness tour, "You know when you go into one of those things that you're gonna fight someone for a year. Every day, toe-to-toe, face-to-face combat. You're gonna wanna kill him and he's gonna wanna kill you. That's what it's all about, depositions. And it takes its toll. But on the other hand, it's still a guy that you...kinda...like—and you know he kinda likes you.

"What it all came down to was principle. [Mike] worked hard for a long time—we all worked hard—and he sacrificed and, okay, he deserved something for it. But what I wanted was the thing itself: my songs...That whole period of my life just seemed to be out of my hands. That's why I started playing music and writing in the first place—to control my life. No way was I gonna let that get away."

One of the most complex—and misunderstood—aspects of the Springsteen story is his relationship with Appel, who has been painted almost universally as a villain in Springsteen articles and Springsteen folklore. And why not? Didn't Springsteen write "The Promise," a mournful, moody track whose melody suggests "Up on the Roof," precisely about his disheartening relationship with Appel?

The truth is that Springsteen probably still likes Appel personally—a view that comes from someone in the Springsteen camp.

In fact, there is much to suggest that Appel was as important a force in Springsteen's pre-Born to Run days as Landau has been since. Where Landau comes across as sensitive, intelligent and rational, Appel appeared loud, unreasonable and dogmatic. He believed Bruce Springsteen was the most important artist in the world, and he wasn't going to be satisfied until everyone recognized the point—including Bruce. He wasn't subtle about spreading the message.

Preceding page: Darkness at the end of the alley, from left, Max Weinberg, Clarence Clemons, Springsteen, Roy Bittan, Steve Van Zandt, Garry Tallent and Danny Frederici.

The problem was that Appel's aspirations finally began to interfere with Bruce's musical vision. His world was turned upside down after *Born to Run*, and he had to re-evaluate everything. The contract was a serious point of dispute, but Springsteen also must have realized instinctively that his goals and Appel's were no longer compatible. He wasn't Elvis and Appel wasn't the Colonel. He wouldn't turn his career over to someone else. As much as the contract, the philosophical differences between Appel and Springsteen caused the split.

On May 28, 1977, Springsteen and Appel finally reached a settlement. The details have never been fully divulged. Appel is said to have won several hundred thousand dollars from Springsteen and CBS for giving up his interest in the artist. Springsteen got control of his publishing and recording. Less than a week after the settlement, he and Landau went into the studio in New York and began working on the *Darkness on the Edge of Town* album.

Though Springsteen wrote his share of good-time rockers during this period—including the classic "Sherry Darling"—his overall

Preceding pages: Bare-breasted encore on the *Darkness* tour; Adele Springsteen lecturing her son for the edification of thousands, 1978; Bruce hoofs it in wintry Monmouth County; portraits from a time tempered by a darker mood. Below, the girls can't help it.

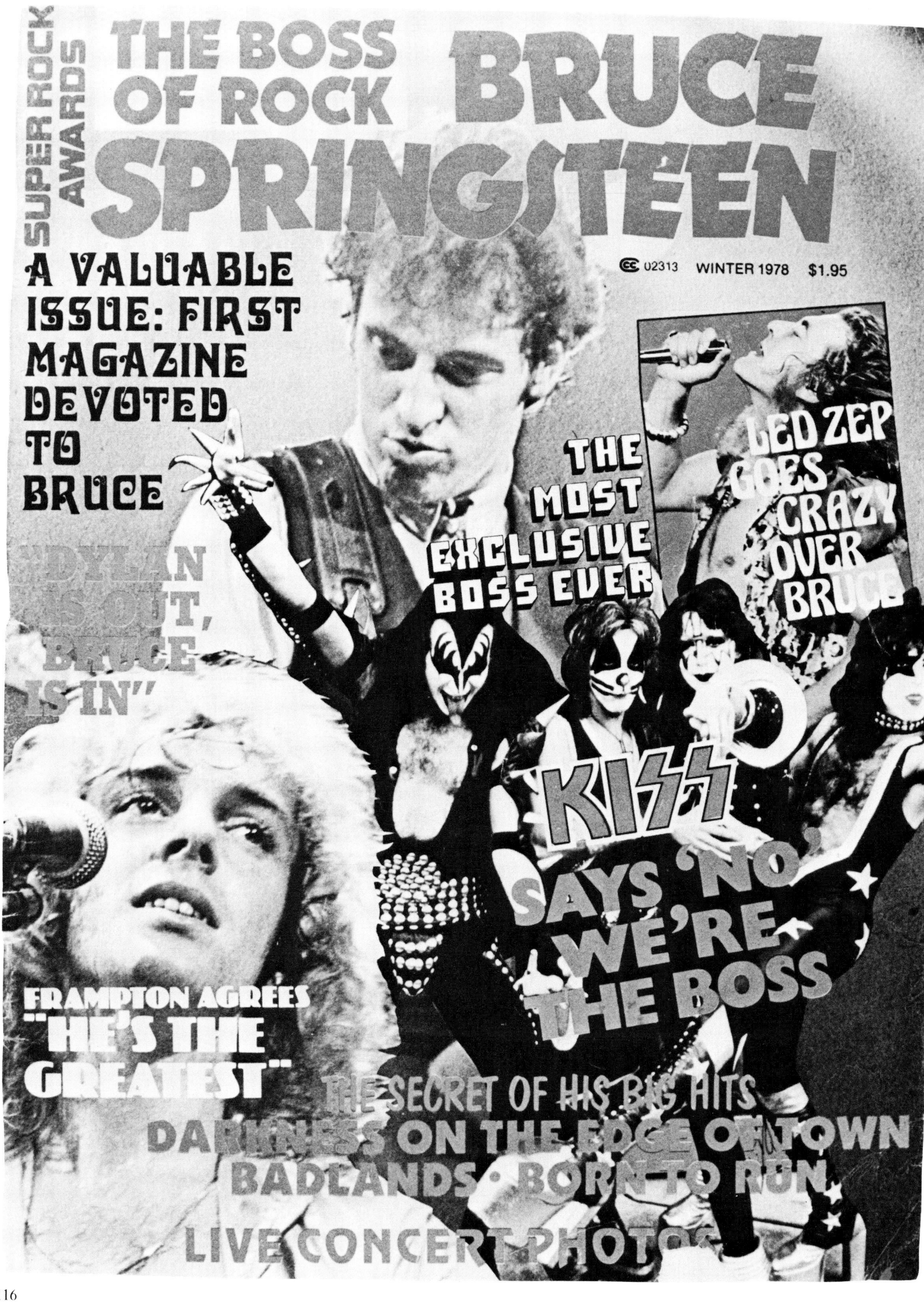
SUPER ROCK AWARDS
THE BOSS OF ROCK
BRUCE SPRINGSTEEN
A VALUABLE ISSUE: FIRST MAGAZINE DEVOTED TO BRUCE
02313 WINTER 1978 $1.95
THE MOST EXCLUSIVE BOSS EVER
LED ZEP GOES CRAZY OVER BRUCE
"DYLAN IS OUT, BRUCE IS IN"
KISS
SAYS 'NO' WE'RE THE BOSS
FRAMPTON AGREES "HE'S THE GREATEST"
THE SECRET OF HIS BIG HITS
DARKNESS ON THE EDGE OF TOWN
BADLANDS · BORN TO RUN
LIVE CONCERT PHOTOS

mood was gloomier, and the songs selected for *Darkness* reflected that mood. While his songs weren't totally devoid of hope, they were enervated and sad. In the searing title track, Springsteen howled with anger and rejection "for wanting things that can only be found/In the darkness on the edge of town"—and never had his band more powerfully echoed his feelings.

Here, in Dylan Thomas' phrase, were "the boys of summer in their ruin," men well into adulthood caught up in the now-joyless rituals of adolescence. Pre-eminent among these songs was the stirring "Racing in the Street," one of Springsteen's personal favorites. The title and chorus played on Martha and the Vandellas' exultant "Dancing in the Streets," but there was little happiness for the aging drivers on the dragstrip, or for their forgotten wives and girlfriends. What's left after youth and its passions have gone? Nothing but to "go down to the sea/And wash these sins off our hands."

Springsteen had always considered himself strong, and he was thrown off by how hard he had been hit—from all sides—after the *Born to Run* success.

About that period, Springsteen has said, "Right after *Born to Run* I asked myself, 'What do I really want?' I figured I better get it straight…[and]…I said, 'I want to be a rocker, a musician, not a rock & roll star.' There's a difference. The bigger you get the more responsibility you have. So you have got to keep constant vigilance. You got to keep your strength up because if you lose it, then you're another jerk who had his picture on the cover."

Like *The Wild, the Innocent, Darkness on the Edge of Town* was a transitional album. Though the rush of loyal Springsteen fans to get the album pushed it into the Top 10 in the summer of 1978, sales didn't keep pace with *Born to Run*. It sold 1.2 million the first year, but has sold only another 500,000 in the years since. That left it in January 1985 about 1.2 million less than *Born to Run* and only 600,000 more than *The Wild, the Innocent and the E Street Shuffle*.

Where *Born to Run* was mixed at symphonic fullness, the sound on *Darkness* was moodier. Songs like "Promised Land" still featured the dense mix of keyboards, guitars and drums, but the solos are short, the players who blew so lustily on *Born to Run* are kept in check. Clarence Clemons' honking sax lines add color, but they don't dominate the last chorus of the songs the way they did on the two previous albums. Very few major rock bands were using the Hammond B-3 organ sound like Danny Federici, and his romantic and sometimes keening melodies are a throwback to the rock music of the '60s. In this sense, the E Street Band are all traditionalists. This album was recorded during a time of stripped down, primitive releases by punk bands like the Ramones, Sex Pistols and the Clash. Yet Springsteen was able to take the trademark vintage sounds from albums like Dylan's *Blonde on Blonde, Mr. Tambourine Man* by the Byrds and the music of the Ronnettes, Junior Walker and Gary U.S. Bonds and make it new and personal. The tempos are sometimes played at dirge pacing, and when the guitars lash out, as they do on "Streets of Fire," they sting. *Darkness* is not a recitation of the great party sounds. That would have to wait until Bruce's mood changed.

While fans could cling to the notes of celebration in "Prove It All Night" and "Badlands"—"It ain't no sin to be glad you're alive"— the more disturbing sides of *Darkness* put off some listeners. Its flashes of guitar virtuosity were less frequent. Perhaps his battle with Appel and the hiatus it had forced on him had shown Springsteen that freedom isn't always a midnight drive away; that so many people feel trapped—not just by their town or their youth or their jobs ("Factory"), but also by their familial responsibilities ("Adam Raised a Cain") and even by their own minds ("Promised Land"). These songs explored more fully basic concerns of the rock & roll form, but did so in a less sentimental, less celebratory mode than before.

That doesn't mean the album was without hope. In the opening song, "Badlands," he spelled out the hardships ("Lights out tonight/ Trouble in the heartland") but still asserted an optimistic vision.

Though *Darkness* lacked the seductive glow of *Born to Run*, it was probably a more consistent set of songs and, above all, an essential step in Springsteen's evolution as an artist. It represented his first step toward a leaner, more accessible writing style. "Factory," for instance, has little of the flashy literary sweep of his early work. But it was a breakthrough—his most successful step yet at conveying a powerful mood with a minimum of words, and an important step in blending personal experience and public comment. Just as "Spirit in

Ronnie Spector greeting the New Jersey delegation.

the Night" was a forerunner of his narratives, "Factory" was the precursor of sparse yet riveting tunes like "Stolen Car" and "Highway Patrolman."

"For me the whole thing [in the album] is just people stretchin' for the light in the darkness, just people tryin' to hold on for the things they believe in the face of the battering from the outside," he said in 1978.

"On the old stuff, there's a lot of characters and groups of people and as it goes along it thins out; people drop by the wayside, until on *Born to Run*, it's essentially two: it's a guy and a girl.

"And then on *Darkness*, there's a lotta times when there's just one. In the end, on the last song, there's just one."

Springsteen understood solitude. Even before *Darkness*, Springsteen had spoken about the importance of keeping trim free of ties.

"Yeah, I like friends, but I'm pretty much by myself out there most of the time," he said. "My father was always like that. I lived with my father twenty years and never once saw a friend come over to the house. Not one time."

Added someone who has been close to Bruce for nearly a decade, "Bruce is very private... very much a loner. I don't mean to say he's lonely. He's not, he's just very much within himself. He loves to get in a car and just drive, sometimes for hours, by himself. There's some kind of peace he finds in that solitude. But he's no Howard Hughes either. He has friends and he enjoys people's company. It's just that he doesn't always need to be in a crowd."

There was some criticism during the *Darkness* period that Springsteen was relying on the same images—cars, night, streets—but Bruce argued that the important thing wasn't the images but the way the characters related to them. He said he was working in a tradition that was well accepted in films.

"The songs are always different to me," he has said. "I became fascinated with John Ford movies, the fact that they were all westerns. I watched the early ones and the late ones. It was fascinating to me how he'd film the same scene—a dance scene or a confrontation—and make it different in every picture.

"There was a lot of continuity in his work. I liked that. You [could then] go back to the previous movie and have a clearer understanding of where he was coming from. What he was saying in this film was changing the shape of what he said in another one."

Jon Landau sees much of *Darkness* as a reaction to Springsteen's experience with *Born to Run*. He said, "That album took eleven months to make. Bruce was absolutely in no rush whatsoever. He had no interest in whether there was anything he could call a single. He was totally committed to making a record that was true to his own feelings. When you consider he had, but didn't use songs like 'Fire' and 'Because the Night,' you've got to assume he didn't really want *Darkness* to be that big a record.

"Bruce was very suspicious about success. If success was what it was like with *Born to Run*, Bruce didn't want that. He didn't want to have one song that could be taken out of context and interfere with what he wanted the album to represent."

Bruce Springsteen's commitment to his concert audiences begins before the show. Where many bands dawdle through their sound checks, Springsteen checks the sound personally at every section of the arena, good seats and bad. Where lots of bands will throw heavily populated parties before they hit the stage, Springsteen has a strict rule forbidding backstage visitors before showtime. It's one of the ways that he keeps his and the band's energies focused on their work and on the spirit of the music that they're about to play.

And as he hit the road in 1978 for the *Darkness* tour, Springsteen seemed more dedicated to keeping that spirit alive than ever before. He seemed to feel a new closeness to his audience. When I talked to him backstage after one of the tour's first shows, in Minneapolis, that dedication was impossible to miss. He seemed different, no longer wrestling with whether he should talk about himself or the music.

He told me backstage in a musty dressing room in Minneapolis, "The general tone of the album tells what it was like the last few years," he said. "It had me up; it had me down. When I was off, though, I never doubted. I never lost track of what I was trying to do.

"The great thing now is to go out there every night and see those kids and get that kind of response. It's like something special with that crowd. In a way, I like to think I was off three years and they were off three years. It's like they were rooting for you. There's a little extra thing that's there now. It's just a little bit more satisfying."

The *Darkness* tour also found Springsteen's raps on stage more honest and playful. During his club days, Springsteen found the raps useful on two levels. When properly delivered, they added an element of theater to the shows. But they also personalized the songs, making it easier for the audience to relate to both him and the music. On the *Born to Run* tour, Springsteen would frequently lead into the Animals' old "It's My Life" with painfully intense stories about his father, painting the older Springsteen as someone whose setbacks left him bitter and unable to see any better life for his son.

After his return the raps became lighter and more embracing.

"I think my mother and father and sister are here tonight," he said during a California concert on the 1978 tour. "For six years, they've been following me around, trying to make me come back home... Every time I come in the house, they say, 'It's not too late, you could still go back to college.'

"But it's funny, 'cause when I was growin' up, there were two things that were unpopular in my house: one was me, the other was my guitar... I remember when I was first playing, my father, like he couldn't figure out what kind of guitar I was playing. He didn't know if it was a Fender guitar or a Gibson guitar... I always remember him sticking his head in the door and saying, 'Turn down that goddamn guitar.'

"He must've thought all that stuff in my room was the same make, because it used to be 'Turn down that goddamn radio' or 'Get that

The intensity of the live shows calls for sports medicine. Springsteen is frequently bandaged, ankle-taped and rubbed with liniment after a marathon concert. Overleaf: The Mighty Max and his simple drum kit; Bruce, drained but not out.

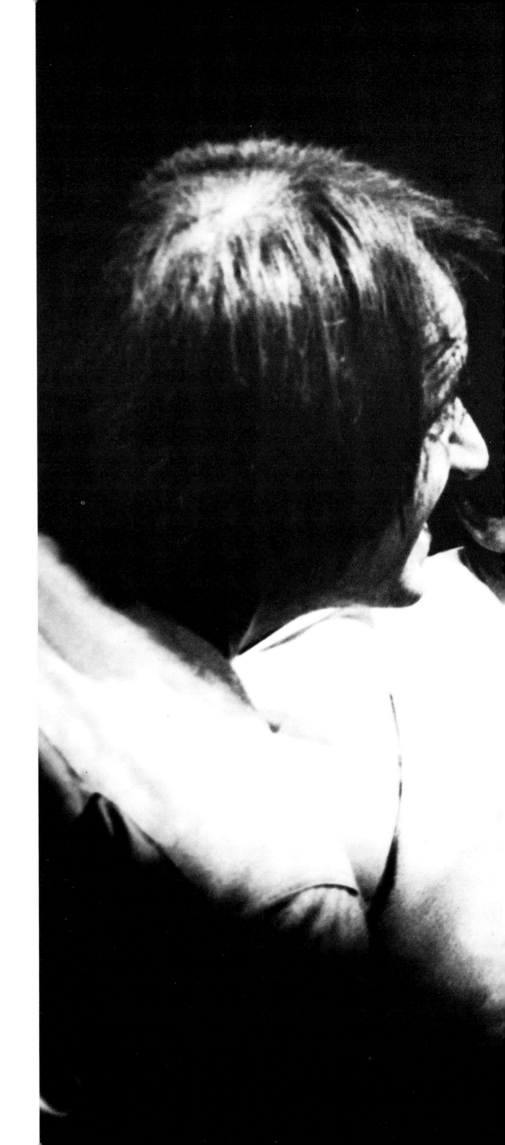

goddamn record off that goddamn stereo.' I couldn't figure it out.

"My father, he used to give me a hard time all the time, he never used to let up. It was always, 'Turn it down, turn it down, turn it down.' So tonight, I've got three million watts. I'm playing a hundred times louder than my stereo ever was—and he comes to see me."

If Springsteen was more comfortable with his past, he was also more comfortable with the present. One reason was Jon Landau, who had become Springsteen's manager.

Landau had wanted to be a rock star himself as a teenager. Born in Brooklyn, he played guitar in a band and was even offered a contract by Columbia Records, but turned it down in favor of college.

While a sophomore at Brandeis University in 1965, Landau began contributing to the early rock magazine *Crawdaddy*. His articles caught the eye of *Rolling Stone*'s Jann Wenner, who asked Landau to contribute to the magazine. The relationship lasted until Landau decided in the mid-'70s to concentrate on record production.

At first, Springsteen looked to Landau chiefly for ideas about music. He credits Landau with helping him focus on the key ideas in songs. Gradually, Springsteen recognized Landau as someone he could trust and someone whose reserved intellectualism was introducing him to books and films he knew little about. As he grew as an artist, Springsteen was naturally curious about things, and Landau helped him explore those interests.

"Bruce's attitude about a manager wasn't just someone who makes deals for him," Landau once explained. "It was more someone who would continue the approach we used in the studio, the exchange of ideas. Bruce sort of knows where he wants to go a lot of the time, and it's my job to try to help him realize those plans. It's not like you go to him and say, 'This is what we're going to do.' It's night and day from that."

Peter Philbin, a former Columbia Records executive, argues that Mike Appel was just the kind of manager Springsteen needed when he was young and struggling, and that Landau is the ideal manager for the post-*Born to Run* Springsteen.

"Jon is not the personality to do what Mike did early, and Mike isn't the personality to do what Jon has done," Philbin said. "Mike put Bruce on the map as much as a manager can and once he was on the map, Jon was able to maximize it. Jon believes in a very quiet, supportive rational approach. With him, it's 'what does Bruce want and need?' With Mike, it was always Mike's show. With Jon, it's Bruce's show. Jon is there to advise and help."

Beyond music, the quality that most impressed Landau during his early meetings with Bruce was the latter's dedication to his craft.

"There was this totally sincere interest in improving the quality of what he did and there was a complete absence of concern about practical success," another associate has said. "Plus, I could see right away that he had the power to inspire—not just in his music, but also

By the late-seventies, Springsteen had laid the "East Coast phenomenon" tag to rest.

in his conversations. I found myself inspired by him. I came away from our earliest meetings thinking, 'This guy is different. There is something going on here.'"

The same thing happened to me. Back in 1974, I was eager to interview Springsteen simply because I appreciated his talent, and I wanted to know what contributed to his artistic vision. But I had a lot of professional detachment as I wove his remarks into a story. I had been conditioned to separate the artist from the individual.

I believed the idealism Springsteen expressed in his early interviews, but I had seen how many other great talents had compromised similar idealism over the years. Maybe the best we could expect in rock was a steady supply of newcomers who would remind us of the idealism before they would succumb to the pressures and temptations of success.

Even after being around him on the Born to Run tour, I kept this separation between Springsteen the artist and the individual. It wasn't until *Darkness* that the depth of Springsteen's dedication became apparent and those of us on the West Coast began to understand why long-time East Coast fans would drive hundreds of miles to see Springsteen in concert.

I had driven ninety miles to see Bruce perform in Santa Barbara on the Born to Run tour, but I had also driven there to see Elvis Costello, John Prine and Talking Heads. It wasn't that big a deal, I simply found Bruce the most satisfying figure in rock at the time, and I wanted to see as many of his concerts as possible while he maintained that spark.

I realized the faith I was beginning to put in Springsteen the December day in 1978 that I drove 400 miles to Tucson, Arizona, to see him in concert. The show was part of a short western swing near the end of the Darkness tour that skipped Los Angeles. On the way to Tucson, I told myself I was just going for entertainment's sake, just to see the show.

As I sat in the arena, however, I began to sense how important Springsteen's music was—both in terms of rock history and to me personally. My first rock hero, like Bruce's, had been Elvis Presley. There was something about Elvis' energy and spirit that made me feel a little more alive in the '50s, that became a symbol of how a teenager like myself could realize his dreams. I didn't think seriously about being a musician myself, though I did buy a black guitar and stand with it in front of the mirror a few times, trying to picture myself in Elvis' place.

The same swell of emotion came to me during Bruce's concert in Tucson. It wasn't as easy to think that anything is possible now that I was in my thirties as it was listening to Elvis back in my teens, but seeing Springsteen push himself so hard on stage and listening to the eloquence of his songs made me forget about doubts and think about my own dreams again.

Springsteen would later make it clear in some songs from *The River* that the trick is guarding against disillusionment is to search

Preceding page: Jackson Browne and Tom Petty join E Streeters for an encore during a M.U.S.E. show at Madison Square Garden, 1979.

for new dreams to replace the ones that have to be discarded. The joy of watching him is that he works so hard every night at living up to his own dreams that it invites you to do the same and to examine what you're doing to see how close you are coming to your own ideals.

I hadn't planned to say hello to Bruce after the show but I ran into a friend from CBS Records backstage who brought me along to the dressing room. Bruce was as warm as ever, and I walked with him to the bus. It was nearly 2 A.M., but he still stopped and chatted with fans. He signed autographs and answered questions for nearly an hour. It was clear from everything he said and did that what he had said about rock & roll giving him a purpose in life, that the music—not the stardom—was his prime motivation, was true.

As I drove back to Los Angeles that night I knew one thing for sure: The important thing about Bruce isn't that he makes you believe in rock & roll or himself. He makes you believe in yourself.

Bruce was off the road for nearly two years after the Darkness tour. Those gaps in his career may be frustrating to his fans, but it's one way that he maintains the quality of his work. Springsteen uses the time to work on new material, but he also steps outside the rock star mold—taking an occasional drive across country, checking out some new bands, catching up on old movies.

Springsteen did interrupt his break from touring in the fall of 1979, when he and the E Streeters played two performances at the No Nukes benefits in New York's Madison Square Garden on September 22nd and 23rd, sponsored by MUSE (Musicians United for Safe Energy). The sets were short by his standards, but from the cries of "Bruuuuuuuce" that were heard during some of the opening acts' performances, many New York fans had clearly come to see him and him alone. Chaka Khan, in fact, wept backstage, believing that the fans were booing her. "Too bad his name isn't Melvin," said Bonnie Raitt as she consoled Khan.

The second night was Springsteen's thirtieth birthday, and the stress of that milestone may have been partially responsible for two of the more uncharacteristically untoward moments of his career. When a birthday cake was brought out to him, he hurled it into the front rows, spattering the patrons and their clothing with icing and sponge cake. In the photographer's pit, he spotted Lynn Goldsmith, with whom he had recently concluded a lengthy affair. Against her wishes, he pulled her onstage—"This is my ex-girlfriend," he told the confused crowd—and roughly tossed her to his roadies, who hustled her out.

Even though the anti-nuclear cause was one that most of Springsteen's audience would embrace, many were still surprised to see Bruce involved in a political project. Though it hadn't surfaced in his music, he was beginning to get more curious about social and political issues. He had read and been deeply moved by *Born on the Fourth of July*, a book by Ron Kovic, who was left a paraplegic by the Vietnam War.

Springsteen's live shows from this period featured rockabilly classics like "Good Rockin' Tonight" and "High School Confidential."

Still, he wasn't planning to enter the New Hampshire primary. With the little that he did know about politics, he realized that politicians have no better a record than rock stars in living up to ideals. Before agreeing to perform, he laid down certain conditions, including that no politicians would be allowed on the stage. He also declined to join the other musicians in outlining his reasons for joining the anti-nuclear movement in the MUSE program.

As Springsteen returned to the studio to work on *The River*, he felt good about the way he had gained control of his music and life. There would still be darkness on the new album. But this time, he'd also find room for the light.

The River, the two-record set released in October 1980, is a deceptive album. On first listening, many of the songs seem too frivolous to stand next to the darker, serious songs. But Springsteen had learned that life is filled with paradoxes, and one of them is that you can experience happiness even in the darkest of times.

"Rock & roll has always been this joy, this certain happiness that is in its way the most beautiful thing in life," he explained during the River tour. "But rock is also about hardness and coldness and being alone. With *Darkness*, it was hard for me to make those things coexist. How could a happy song like 'Sherry Darling' coexist with 'Darkness on the Edge of Town?'

"I wasn't ready for some reason within myself to feel those things. It was too confusing, too paradoxical. But I finally got to the place where I realized life had paradoxes, a lot of them, and you've got to live with them."

By accepting the paradoxes of life, Springsteen was able to place songs as different as "Independence Day" and "Out in the Street" on the same record. (Indeed, he reportedly had been ready to issue a single record set entitled "The Ties that Bind" a year earlier, only to add some darker material after penning "The River.") His cottoning to more festive songs marked a particularly important break-through. Before, Bruce had turned to such oldies as Jackie DeShannon's "When You Walk in to the Room" to lighten up the in-concert mood. Now he had a sheaf of his own upbeat rockers to choose from, songs that owed much of their sound to the music that had first stirred their composer. "Ramrod"—a more optimistic "Racing in the Street"—swayed with the energy of "Sea Cruise" or Fredd Cannon's "Palisades Park." Springsteen acknowledged that "Sherry Darling" was rooted in such frat-rock classics as "Farmer John" and "Double Shot of My Baby's Love." But whatever the sources, *The River* simply brimmed with marvelously crafted rock & roll songs, full of joy and release: "I'm a Rocker," "Crush on You" and "Out in the Street" never failed to delight their listeners.

Even with his new outlook, Springsteen almost left "Out in the Street" off the LP. "I wasn't gonna put it on the album because it's all idealism. It's about people being together and sharing a certain

A typical show during the *"River"* tour in 1980-81 featured many songs from that double album *plus* large chunks from *Born to Run* and *Darkness on the Edge of Town.*

feeling. I know [the feeling] is real, but it's hard to see sometimes. You go out in the street, and there's a chance you get hit over the head or mugged. The song's not realistic in a way, but there's something very real at the heart of it."

More than resolving those paradoxes, the album reflected a change from the solitary stance of *Darkness* to an acknowledgement of the need for people. In his thirties, Springsteen was feeling a conflict between independence and responsibility. Several tunes talked about entering or leaving marriages.

In several interviews in the mid-'70s, Springsteen had said how too many possessions or even a family can sidetrack a person by making him more worried about protecting what he has than in searching for more.

"I throw out almost everything I ever own," he told *Melody Maker*'s Ray Coleman in 1975. "I don't believe in collecting anything. The less you have to lose the better you are, because the more chances you'll take. The more you've got, the worse off you get."

About children, he added, "I couldn't bring up kids. I couldn't handle it. I mean it's too heavy, it's too much. A kid—like you better be ready for them. I'm so far off that track. I'm so far out of line, that

Roy Bittan, Jon Landau, Springsteen, unidentified, and Max Weinberg listening to playback during a *River* session.

it would be disastrous. I don't understand it. I just don't see why people get married. It's so strange. I guess it's a nice track, but not for me."

The River, though, showed Springsteen addressing emotional commitments, "the ties that bind," in a more positive way than he had before. The man who seemed afraid of getting trapped now could unashamedly sing "little girl, I wanna marry you." Once, he had shied away from recording such romantic compositions as "Fire" or "Because the Night"; now, he declared "I would drive all night/Just to buy you some shoes." *Darkness* had described grown men refusing to acknowledge their new, adult responsibilities; on *The River,* shouldering the burdens of life is seen as heroism, whether it's the man with a wife and baby in "The River" or the search for true love in the under-appreciated "Two Hearts." And neglecting the responsibility to be compassionate brings troubled thoughts to the narrator of "Wreck on the Highway." Bruce was reaching for an "everyday sense" in his songs.

"To me, the type of things that people do that make their lives heroic are a lot of times very small, little things," he has said. "Little things that happen in a kitchen or something, or between a husband and a wife, or between them and their kids. It's a grand experience, but it's not always big. There's plenty of room for those kinds of victories and I think the records have that."

The album's title song defined Springsteen's new direction—a classic outline of someone who has to re-adjust his dreams quickly. The character faces life as it is, not a world of his imagination:

•

THEN I GOT MARY PREGNANT
AND, MAN, THAT WAS ALL SHE WROTE
AND FOR MY 19TH BIRTHDAY I GOT A UNION
   CARD AND A WEDDING COAT
WE WENT DOWN TO THE COURTHOUSE
AND THE JUDGE PUT IT ALL TO REST
NO WEDDING DAY SMILES, NO WALK DOWN
   THE AISLE
NO FLOWERS, NO WEDDING DRESS

•

Even though it was a two-record set, *The River* was his biggest hit to date, thanks in part to the success of "Hungry Heart," Springsteen's first Top 10 single, and the enormous success of Springsteen's year-long tour that began in October 1980. The LP sold a phenomenal 1.6 million copies by Christmas—and would surely have sold more had not one of the album's weakest tracks, "Fade Away," been released as the second single. Nevertheless, *The River* and the extensive U.S. tour that immediately followed its release made Springsteen not just a critical but also popular favorite with rock & roll fans across the country. No longer was he seen as merely an East Coast critical phenomenon. Massive commercial success was now in his grasp, his for the asking…but once again, Springsteen would reject the easier road.

In the late spring and summer of 1981, Springsteen took his juggernaut to Europe, where he hadn't played since his ill-fated shows in 1975. By all accounts, he was received with an enthusiasm comparable to that of his stateside audiences. Offstage, though, he found that many people there thought of America as a land fueled by greed and self-interest. He started poring through books on America history—and pondered the gap between the country's ideals and its direction. His reading of Southern writers like Flannery O'Connor may have reinforced the strong sense of place and almost cinematic feel of his song lyrics.

He returned to America for a second series of shows, including the first shows of any kind at New Jersey's new venue, the 20,000-seat Brendan Byrne Arena in East Rutherford. Predictably, the home-town boy's return was greeted with particular joy, especially when he played a surprise cover, Tom Waits' "Jersey Girl." He even journeyed down to Red Bank, New Jersey, where he and the E Streeters inaugurated Clarence Clemons' club, Big Man's West, with a sweat-drenched set of oldies like "Around and Around," "You Can't Sit Down" and "Jole Blon," the song that Springsteen had sung with Gary U.S. Bonds on the latter's comeback record.

But for all Bruce's buoyancy, the arena shows had some darker underpinnings. Bruce's raps grew longer and more poignant. Perhaps confused by a newer, younger audience that knew him only from the *The River*, Springsteen started asking for quiet before his more serious songs: a solemn solo version of "This Land Is Your Land," his tribute to Elvis, "Bye, Bye Johnny" (a speeded-up version of which appears on the B-side of the "Born in the U.S.A." single) and the unforgettable "Trapped," plucked off a Jimmy Cliff cassette Bruce dug up in Europe.

The setting was still more sobering on August 20th, when Bruce played the first of a series of shows at the Los Angeles Memorial Sports Arena. Opening night was a benefit for the Vietnam Veterans of America Foundation, and the show began not with a typical Springsteen crowd-rouser, but with a brief talk by the foundation's president, Robert Muller. As wheelchair-ridden vets lined the stage, Muller spoke of the pain of the veteran and of his joy that rock & roll could bring disparate factions together under a musical banner. The packed house listened with remarkable attentiveness.

With that as a prelude, Bruce and his band launched into a shuddering version of Creedence Clearwater Revival's "Who'll Stop the Rain," a banshee cry against governmental hypocrisy and distrust. That night he played his usual show of superb music—but he also talked to his audience perhaps more than he'd ever done before. He didn't have to ask for quiet—the mere force of his words hushed the crowds as he spoke of the agony of so many of his countrymen, cut off forever from the American Dream, people like the protagonist of "Bye Bye Johnny":

The *River* Tour ran for some 139 shows over eleven and a half months. Springsteen seasoned his last three-hour set with "Mony Mony", the Tommy James and the Shondells' hit dropped into his Mitch Ryder medley.

THEY FOUND HIM SLUMPED UP
AGAINST THE DRAIN
WITH A WHOLE LOT OF NOTHIN'
RUNNING THROUGH HIS VEINS
WELL BYE BYE JOHNNY
JOHNNY BYE BYE
YOU DIDN'T HAVE TO DIE
YOU DIDN'T HAVE TO DIE

•

When Springsteen returned to the recording studio to begin work on his next album, little seemed to have changed. As usual, Springsteen had no problem coming up with new songs. He wrote them in his New Jersey home and recorded his spare demo versions on a four-track tape machine. Then he played the demos for the band and helped them work out the songs' arrangements.

Studio time tends to run on for the finicky Springsteen. This time, though, his dissatisfaction with the band's versions of his songs ran deeper. He wasn't troubled by the band's work; there just seemed to be some mood in his newer material that was getting lost in the translation from demo to performance. It wasn't just Springsteen who sensed it, either; other members of the band also noticed it. Bruce recalled later, "[it] was different from the stuff I'd done before—and I didn't know what it was."

The demos seemed more intimate, more haunting; Springsteen felt that they reflected the loneliness and uncertainty that was at the heart of the songs. A daring idea took shape in his head: Why not just release the demos as an LP?

Why not? Well, for starters, the technical problems alone were enormous. Springsteen had recorded the songs on a cassette tape that he'd carried around in his pants pocket for days; the wear and tear on the tape combined with its already primitive recording quality was enough to give ace engineer-producer Chuck Plotkin some major headaches trying to make it sound good enough to release.

And what about the commercial considerations? With *The River*, Springsteen had become America's Number One rock & roller; how would his fans react to his putting out a record of folk songs? Strictly regimented playlists were the norm on rock radio stations in 1982. What if nobody played the record on the air? It had taken years for Bruce to build his career to this point, but the release of this record could shatter that momentum overnight—especially since he wasn't planning to tour behind it. How could he do it?

No matter: He did. He called the album *Nebraska* and released it with little fanfare. As they had in the past, some stations got copies of the record before the official release date and started playing it. One such station, Cleveland's WMMS, reported that listener reaction was strongly mixed. When a telegram arrived from CBS

The *Nebraska* demo tape traveled around in Bruce's shirt pocket for a couple of weeks.

ordering the station to stop playing the record, WMMS's program director joked that CBS should thank him, not spank him, for featuring such an out-of-the-ordinary record.

Nebraska was instantly hailed by the critics as a masterpiece of boldness and individuality, a statement from Springsteen that he wouldn't play the star-making games that so many artists had fallen into before him. Some old comparisons were revived, as a few writers described *Nebraska* as the most radical change in style by a major artist since Dylan went electric.

Nebraska may stand as Springsteen's most heroic moment. It may also be the album of his that will outlive the others, because of the timelessness of its style and its refusal to run away from the anguish of the human spirit.

Part history lesson and part social outcry, *Nebraska* offers an uncompromising portrait of the way forces, be it the home or formal institutions, strangle some people so completely that they lose their will entirely or strike back savagely.

Springsteen has described the album in these terms: "The record was just basically about people being isolated from their jobs, from their friends, from their family, from their fathers, their mothers, not being connected to anything that's going on, your government. And I think when that happens, there's just a whole breakdown. When you lose that sense of the community, there's some spiritual breakdown that occurs. You just get shot off somewhere where nothin' really matters."

Though frequent references to unemployment gave the album a timely ring during a period when unemployment was reaching alarming proportions, Springsteen avoided topical arguments to remind us that hard times are always present for some people.

In the chilling title track, Springsteen recounted loosely the story of Charles Starkweather, who was executed in 1959 after he and a girlfriend, Caril Fugate, went on a ten-murder spree. Asked by a judge to explain his actions, the song's central character leaves us

Brian Zaremski of Hanover Park, Illinois, an MTV Grand Prize winner, accepts a guitar from Bruce. He went on tour as a roadie and lifted amps just like the pros.

with a harrowing thought about how perverse a tortured soul can become. Showing no remorse, he simply underscored the emptiness of his life by saying, "At least for a while, sir, me and her/We had us some fun."

"Johnny 99" tells about someone shoved into a tragic situation even before he knows what has happened to him. One of two songs on the album later recorded by Johnny Cash, it includes the lines:

•

NOW JUDGE I GOT DEBTS NO HONEST MAN
   COULD PAY
THE BANK WAS HOLDIN' MY MORTGAGE AND
   THEY WAS TAKIN' MY HOUSE AWAY
NOW I AIN'T SAYIN' THAT MAKES ME AN
   INNOCENT MAN
BUT IT WAS MORE'N ALL THIS THAT PUT
   THAT GUN IN MY HAND.

•

If Springsteen's music seemed personal before, he was singing even more directly to his audience on *Nebraska*. His guitar playing, clean and elemental, isn't meant to shut down Ry Cooder or Richard Thompson. He gets the most emotional mileage that he can from the simple chording. Mood is the important thing, and it's conveyed

Bruce interacts with the front row fanatics, 1975.

powerfully by the lone guitar and forlorn harmonica. The pervasive Woody Guthrie feel is offset with a few rock and country sounds and the occasional gospel yelps. Yet the listener can't help but think what all these solitary tunes might be like with a full-blown E Street treatment. They would be different, obviously, but nothing can dilute this verbal energy and vivid lyricism.

Though Springsteen's singing demonstrated an increased sensitivity, his songwriting remained the album's outstanding feature. He was able to capture the most complex human emotions in simple stories that seemed as casual as conversation. These stories didn't seem part of rock & roll or show business; they seemed like accounts that had been passed down the street.

Great albums don't come out of a vacuum. Asked during the Born in the U.S.A. tour if he had ever gone through another period as trying as the one after the *Time* and *Newsweek* covers and the Appel lawsuit, Springsteen responded, "Yeah, I was going through some things around the *Nebraska* album, but it's not stuff I really want to go into. It was just kinda growin' up, growin' into the particular shoes I was wearing."

On one level, *Nebraska* was an extension of the social concerns Springsteen began expressing during the River tour. He wanted to go behind the headlines and statistics to examine the lives of people who had been pushed to desperate extremes. He had always been interested in the outcast, but he realized there was a layer in society far more distanced than anything he had touched on in his early songs.

The stark, solitary tone of *Nebraska* also represents a break from the communal spirit of his music—here was one person speaking to you. Springsteen's lifestyle during this period was solitary, and it made sense for him to speak on this one-to-one basis.

Bruce has seen Terrence Malick's film *Badlands*, about Starkweather and Fugate, and he had read a novel about the pair. In their story he saw a symbol of the alienation that he wanted to describe.

"It just seemed to be a mood that I was in at the time," he has said. "I was renting a house on this reservoir, and I didn't go out much, and for some reason I just started to write…I was interested in writing kind of smaller than I had been, writing with just detail…I guess my influences at the time were the movie and these stories I was reading by Flannery O'Connor."

"The details in the songs are always secondary, which doesn't mean they aren't important to get right," he has said. "But detail alone is just detail. I have a lot of songs sitting in my notebook that are full of detail, but missing the emotion which ties the whole thing together and breathes life into it.

"The emotion is what makes a song real and breathes life into it. The detail gives you the grit of living. That's important, but the emotion gives you the feel of living. That's what I find in songs like 'Nebraska,' 'My Hometown,' 'Stolen Car,' 'Wreck on the Highway.' A lot of those songs are connected. Take 'Adam Raised a Cain,' 'Independence Day,' 'My Father's House'—if you play those three songs together, you'll see somebody grow up."

For Bruce Springsteen, *Nebraska* was a watershed album. Perhaps he had proved to himself that he really could avoid all the traps of the rock & roll lifestyle, the traps of wealth, self-indulgence and isolation that had destroyed his first idol, Elvis. He had taken control over his career and emerged with his sanity and self-respect intact.

Back in the studio, he wrote and recorded songs as prolifically as ever and with increasing energy. By some estimates he wrote and recorded upwards of sixty songs in the process of making his new record. He drove cross-country with a friend of his, meeting people and checking out new cities. He played bits and pieces of the new record for friends like Bob Seger and Jimmy Iovine.

Clearly, this man was excited. He started hopping onstage frequently during shows at Asbury Park's Stone Pony, playing songs like "Oh Carol," "Dirty Water" by the Standells or ZZ Top's "I'm Bad, I'm Nationwide." He started dating a young college student who ran the hatcheck at Clemons' club. It was as if he couldn't wait to get the record out and get on the road. And neither could his fans. Word started to emerge of an album entitled *Born in the U.S.A.*

But being Bruce, he fussed to the end. He changed the album's cover at the last minute, replacing a photograph of his frontside with one of his backside and added a track, "No Surrender," even after the listening session at his record label. "If you don't like the record," he told the Columbia execs with a smile, *"Don't tell me!"* Still, he made what for him were some unprecedented decisions. He would appear in promotional videos for the record, and he would allow an outside producer, Arthur Baker, to create special remixes of the LP's singles. While Springsteen was faithful to the roots of rock & roll, he wasn't about to become a dinosaur.

That attitude was apparent from the start. All you had to do was listen to the album's first single, released a week before the LP itself: "Dancing in the Dark." This didn't sound like a Bruce Springsteen song. To some, its synthesizer hook recalled Rod Stewart's "Young Turks", and its humongous drum sound owed more to hip-hop music than to Phil Spector. Even the lyrics were less complex than Bruce's had been before. "Dancing in the Dark" was just a rock song you could dance to, and while it might not have been the Springsteen buff's favorite song, it shot to the top of the charts.

There is a sense of lost opportunities and hard times running through several tunes in *Born in the U.S.A.* that recall the stark emotional landscapes of *Nebraska,* yet the characters in these new songs don't seem as desperate as those on the earlier LP. One reason is the album's brighter sound. Working again with the E Street Band, Springsteen adapted some of the mainstream traces of '80s rock, including synthesizers and a peppy, aerobics-conscious beat.

The title track opens the album with a rousing anthem tailor-made for concerts. It's no wonder fans hold their arms in the air in salute as he sings it. However, the lyrics suggest a different mood:

As 1984 began, there were rumors of an album of upbeat rock songs on the way, as well as a video featuring Bruce and even a *dance mix* single. By year's end Born in the U.S.A.'s success and Springsteen's new video exposure made people look at him in public as if he were "Santa Claus and the Easter Bunny."

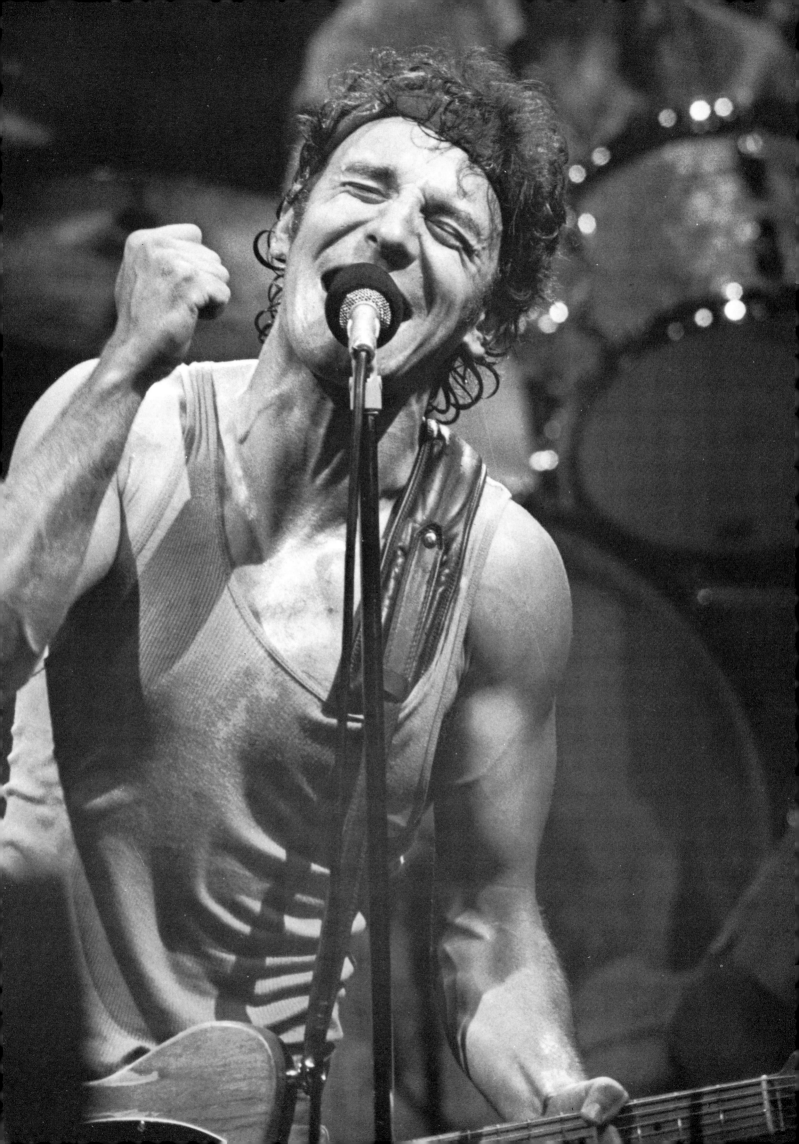

BORN DOWN IN A DEAD MAN'S TOWN
THE FIRST KICK I TOOK WAS WHEN I HIT THE
   GROUND
YOU END UP LIKE A DOG THAT'S BEEN BEAT
   TOO MUCH
'TILL YOU SPEND HALF YOUR LIFE JUST
   COVERING UP.

The song is a compassionate look at the blue-collar generation that bore the brunt of America's Vietnam involvement—many of whom lived through the nightmare of that war only to return home to a bleak future. It's one of the most strident pieces of social commentary ever to become a Top 10 single in America.

The overall sound was clearer, less bombastic than it had ever been. He forsook the much-copied piano and glockenspiel keyboard attack that Jon Landau had brought him and incorporated more synthesizer textures into the band's fabric. With guitarist Steve Van Zandt flitting in and out of the studio, the keyboards became more prominent, and Clemons' saxophone, so tied to a particular rock &

Working class heroes: Bob Seger joins Bruce for an encore during the *River* tour.

roll era, was de-emphasized. Weinberg, who'd been forced to seek treatments for tendonitis in his hands and whose time-keeping skills had been criticized by Springsteen, played more confidently than ever.

As a whole, the album spanned a variety of moods. Not since "For You," when he sung of "that medal you wore on your chest/ You know how it always got in the way," had Springsteen been more blatantly erotic than in "I'm On Fire"; yet that song rested quite comfortably on the same side with the deceptive bravado of the easy-going rocker "Darlington County." Springsteen had written "Cover Me" for Donna Summer, but she'd picked "Protection" instead; his version of the former bristled with taut terror. And while "I'm Goin' Down" might be the album's most tenacious rocker, "Downbound Train" recaptured most forcefully the lonely wounded outcry that was at the heart of "Nebraska." On Side 2, "No Surrender" starts off as a classic rock statement of independence, complete with the full-throttle energy associated with the *Born to Run* days. But the song also reflects on the struggle to regain lost innocence and desire. That song—and "Bobby Jean"—are affectionate tips of the hat to Bruce's continuing friendship with Van Zandt. The album's most haunting number was "My Hometown," which recalls the wistful style of "Independence Day." It's about a couple whose town (and future) have been ravaged by the shifting technology of post-industrial America. At an age in life when it's especially frightening to sever ties with your roots, the couple is finally thinking about moving on.

On a larger scale, the song—and much of the album—examines the responsibilities of citizenship. Just as the couple in "My Hometown" needs to re-evaluate its place, Springsteen suggests that the country needs to examine its traditional values and allegiances to see which of them still apply.

For Springsteen, though, perseverance was key. "I guess it is a kind of thing where you face the loss of those things I wrote about in *Nebraska* and somehow you still keep going. I don't know sometimes. It's not intellectual or knowing the answers...it's just some primitive drive that pushes you forward. It's something you don't understand...it's a mystery. As it should be. It's just part of the mystery of life."

The album was a blockbuster. It raced up the charts to Number One, spent months in second place behind Prince's *Purple Rain,* then retook the top spot early in 1985. Sales through May 1985 were 6.5 million in the U.S. alone. The message of *Nebraska* had been spread to a huge audience.

The Born in the U.S.A. tour was a masterful blend of the *Nebraska* and *Born in the U.S.A.* material. Opening in St. Paul, Minnesota on June 29, 1984, Springsteen spotlighted several of the *Nebraska* songs in a mostly acoustic stretch that worked well in the arena settings. The biggest adjustment for long-time Springsteen fans was getting used to the absence of guitarist Steve Van Zandt.

Van Zandt explained his departure: "One of the reasons I left the [Asbury] Jukes to join Bruce's band was I didn't want the responsi-

bility and pressure of running a band and fighting with all the club owners any more. I also didn't want the focus on me. It was easier to just lay back and watch someone else take over on stage.

"Eventually, though, you get a bit older and you feel a certain need to justify your existence, I guess. With me, I think I realized I may have been relying a little too much on my life with Bruce. I gradually started thinking about what I'd like to say in my own album."

Bruce felt the loss of Van Zandt, personally and professionally, but he respected his friend's desire to make his own statements and thought Van Zandt made two terrific albums. They remain close friends, and Bruce brought Steve on stage for the second encore when the tour reached the Brendan Byrne Arena in New Jersey's Meadowlands in 1984. They stood reunited at the microphone, sharing the vocal on "Two Hearts" and on Dobie Gray's 1973 hit, "Drift Away." Springsteen and Van Zandt embraced at the end of the song, and Bruce launched into "Born to Run."

The Born in the U.S.A. tour was full of surprises.

Besides inviting veteran rocker Nils Lofgren to take Van Zandt's place on guitar, Springsteen also made his first change in the band line-up in years, adding Patti Scialfa, who had formerly appeared with the Asbury Jukes, as a backup singer.

Another surprise: a muscular Springsteen. The junkfood diet had been replaced with more careful eating habits and he worked out regularly, running up to six miles a day. He even had a full-time trainer on the road with him.

Third, Springsteen finally appeared in a video—though not without considerable angst. He engaged the services of director Jeff Stein, who did some filming with Bruce right before the beginning of the tour. Springsteen, however, wasn't pleased with the results, so Brian DePalma was hired at the last minute to film an in-concert but lip-synced video of "Dancing in the Dark." In the view of many, this video was able to do something that had never been done before: make Springsteen look artificial, contrived and uncomfortable in a concert setting. It had all the warmth and sincerity of a deodorant commercial—yet it proved immensely popular with MTV viewers. Another concert video was made for "Born in the U.S.A.," this one directed by John *(The Return of the Secaucus Seven)* Sayles. Again Bruce lip-synced.

On September 18, Springsteen's name was injected into the 1984 presidential campaign, when President Reagan suggested at a campaign rally in Hammontown, New Jersey, that he and Springsteen had similar views about America and its future. "America's future rests in a thousand dreams inside your hearts," Reagan said. "It rests in the message of hope in songs of a man so many young Americans admire: New Jersey's own Bruce Springsteen. And helping you make those dreams come true is what this job of mine is all about."

It's easy to picture how the Reagan reference came about. A speech writer on the outlook for a local angle saw the New Jersey stop on the President's itinerary and threw in the Springsteen reference. It happens all the time.

Springsteen's first reaction was that it was such obvious exploitation that he didn't need to respond. "He felt his music spoke for itself," explained someone who works closely with Bruce. "But the more he thought about it, the more he felt it was important to speak up."

In addition, the aide suggested, Springsteen was worried that people who weren't familiar with his music were going to put together several references—including the Reagan remarks and the *Born in the U.S.A.* album title—and get a superficial impression of him and his music.

In Pittsburgh—the first date after the President's speech—Springsteen disassociated himself from Reagan's remarks, noting sarcastically that the President must not have listened to the *Nebraska* album. When Democrats took the Pittsburgh comments as sign of a Mondale endorsement, Springsteen instructed Jon Landau to deny the existence of any endorsement.

In his second Pittsburgh concert, Springsteen took a more decisive political step. He dedicated a song to the United Steelworkers of America's Local 1397, which has been described as the most activist steel local in the country, and donated $10,000 to the union's food bank program. In subsequent tour stops Springsteen saluted local

Preceding page: newcomers Patti Scialfa (head down, third from left), who had sung with the Asbury Jukes, and guitarist Nils Lofgren (second from right) with the usual suspects. Left: Why moonlight at car washes when your album sells seven million copies? Below: the band behind the band.

food groups, allowing them to set up information booths in arena lobbies.

He also made some pointed remarks when introducing songs. In Oakland, California, Springsteen introduced "Reason to Believe" by saying, "Here's a song about blind faith. That is always a dangerous thing, whether it's your girlfriend"—speaking good-naturedly, then more pointedly—"or if it's in your government."

On the day of the first Oakland show, a Springsteen associate said, "Bruce is at a crossroads now where he is thinking about the connection between what he writes and the larger world. I think what you're seeing in these shows is him trying to find a way to make that connection in a way that's comfortable for him.

"What Reagan did put him on the spot . . . It made him think about what he wanted to do beyond just playing music. Rather than get embroiled with personalities and endorsing candidates, the thing that seems to make the most sense for him is to keep it more personal. That's what he's exploring now in encouraging people to get behind activities like the food banks."

One of the things that pleased Springsteen most about the Born in the U.S.A. tour was the way the audience accepted the *Nebraska* songs. For many, those songs were the highlight of the show. His vision of rock as inspiration had evolved from simply trying to inspire the audience to search for their own potential to encouraging them to accept more responsibility for those less fortunate than they.

Dora Kirby, one of his mother's two sisters, told me during my visit to Freehold in 1984, "You know, when I see Bruce on stage, I always get the idea that he's preaching. The kids don't know what he's doing, but I can see that he's telling them that they can do the same thing that he has—that they can make something of themselves if they work at it."

On a personal level, Springsteen showed that he was up to the increased career pressures. In a *Rolling Stone* interview with Kurt Loder, Springsteen spoke about getting distracted by fame. "You see it happens to so many people. Elvis' case must have been tremendously difficult. Because, I mean, I feel the difference between selling a million records and selling 3 million—I feel a difference out on the street.

"I believe that the life of a rock & roll band will last as long as you look down into the audience and can see yourself, and your audience looks up at you and can see themselves—and as long as those reflections are human, realistic ones. The biggest gift that your fans can give you is just treatin' you like a human being, because anything else dehumanizes you.

"And that's one of the things that has shortened the life spans, both physically and creatively, of some of the best rock & roll musicians—that cruel isolation. If the price of fame is that you have to be isolated from the people you write for, then that's too fuckin' high a price to pay."

You could see the difference between the old Springsteen audience and the new one during his show at the Greensboro Coliseum in January 1985. The 15,500 fans were on their feet, dancing in the dark, and yelling with all the intensity associated with his shows over the years as Bruce and the E Street Band raced through the opening number, "Born in the U.S.A." The fans thrust their arms in the air—just like Bruce—and they cheered his every move. They seemed to be right in step, maybe too much so.

The average age of the fan in the coliseum was probably sixteen, and there was a much higher percentage of girls than ever before. These fans weren't just cheering at the end of every song, they were shrieking during the songs and during the raps between songs. They shrieked when Bruce was serious and they shrieked when Bruce was just fooling around.

I noticed that the three teenage girls squeezed into the two seats on my right seemed to scream the loudest whenever Bruce started dancing or—better yet—turned his back to the audience. At intermission, I asked them what they liked best about Bruce. Replied one girl, fourteen: "His butt."

But what did all this mean to Springsteen?

On stage, he worked as hard as ever. He didn't take the audience for granted and didn't seem thrown by the shrieking. He still seemed to be reaching for the promised land of his rock & roll vision.

Midway through the set, he went into a lengthy rap about accepting responsibility that was as endearing as any of his songs:

"I used to think that once I got out of town, I was never going to come back, but as I got older, I'd come home off the road and...drive back down into town and still see some of my old friends and see what their lives were like and what they were doing. I realized that I would always carry a part of that town with me no matter where I went or what I did.

"When I was a kid, I think I was afraid of belonging to something because if you admit you belong to something that means you've got some responsibility. If you're going to stand up and say, 'I'm an American,' that means you've got some responsibility to America... [cheers] In this country, we've got plenty of things to be proud of and plenty of things to be ashamed of.

"Unless you look at both, unless you look at the bad stuff, there's no way it's going to get better. Tonight, when you go out into the lobby, you're going to see some folks trying to hold up their end of their responsibility to their community—the Food Bank of Northwest North Carolina.

"Every year, 20 percent of all the food that gets produced in the United States gets wasted or thrown away, and meanwhile in every city there are people going hungry, old folks whose social security checks don't get them through the month. They are people who the theory of economics ain't trickling on down to. What a food bank does is get them food. They need your support. Sometimes it seems like people going hungry is something that happens a long ways away. It's hard to believe it happens in a country so rich as ours. That's something we ought to be ashamed of."

He followed with "My Hometown," perhaps the most affecting

ballad he has written.

Listening to the song, I couldn't imagine being any more touched in a concert, and I had experienced a lot of great moments in rock & roll: the threatening presence of the Rolling Stones in 1969, the triumphant return of Elvis Presley to live performances the same year, the celebration at Creedence Clearwater's Royal Albert Hall shows in 1971, David Bowie's unnerving "Ziggy Stardust" tour in 1972, Bob Dylan's glorious reunion with the Band in 1974.

But no one has moved me as consistently as Springsteen. There was the unforgettable night during the Born to Run tour when he fought so hard at the Roxy in Los Angeles to prove to a skeptical industry audience that he was every bit as good as all the critics had said. There was the night in 1978 in Tucson, plus the Vietnam Veterans benefit at the Los Angeles Sports Arena. Maybe three dozen shows in all, and I can't remember a time when I didn't feel enriched.

But the Greensboro show—seemingly just another night on a long, exhausting tour—matched any of them. Springsteen still works as hard as he did the first or tenth or twenty-fifth time I saw him. More important, he continues to grow in surprising, crucial ways.

A symbolic moment in the show was when he sang "Glory Days," a good-natured slap at the way we glamorize the past. Rock & roll has its glory days syndrome, especially among people who were rock fanatics in the '50s or '60s, but now feel alienated from the music. They see today's teenagers obsessed with British swashbucklers like Duran Duran or the ear-shattering assault of Twisted Sister and feel that rock has passed them by—or, more pointedly, let them down.

Springsteen is different. He renews your faith each time. Maybe the best thing about Springsteen is that he keeps convincing his audience that the glory days are right now.

I never thought we'd see another figure in American rock as embracing as Elvis, but Springsteen has become that figure. When he sang Elvis' old "Follow That Dream," written by Ben Weisman and Fred Wise for the 1961 movie of the same name, he relit that torch in Greensboro.

Bruce gave it a prayerful edge on stage, slowing the tempo and changing some of the words. The chorus was identical, however. Two decades apart, Elvis and Bruce both advised their audiences to follow "that dream" wherever it led and to follow it "to find the love you need."

Bruce laughed in the dressing room when I mentioned the girl liking his butt. "Did she really say that?" he asked. "That's great." Yes, he said, he noticed the difference in the audiences these days. The crowds in some of the cities didn't even recognize "Born to Run." But Bruce didn't seem nervous about the changes. The whole idea, he said, is to reach people.

Bruce was sitting alone on a couch in what was normally a team

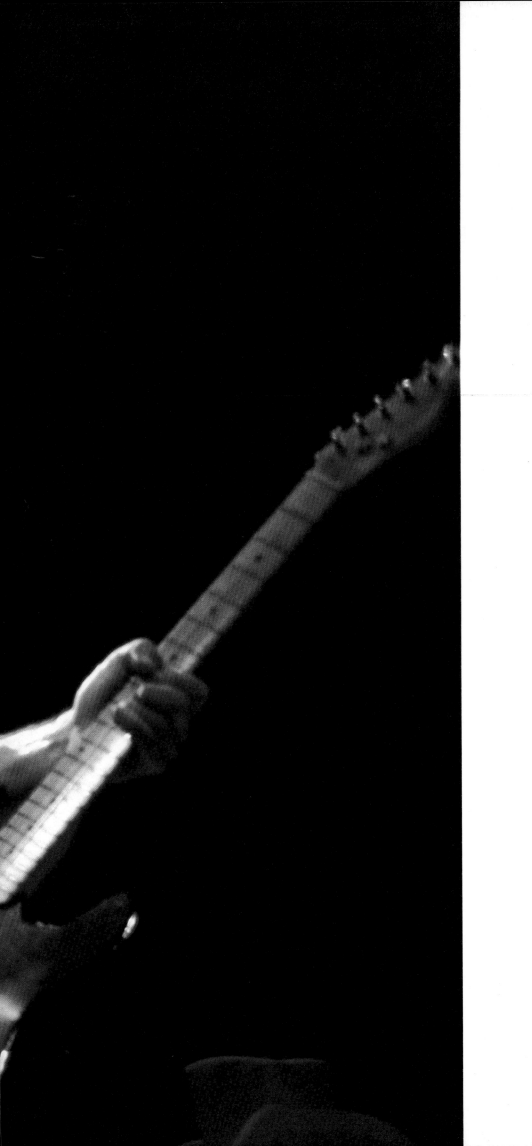

locker room. He smiled warmly, but looked tired. He didn't look like he had the strength to walk to the van that would take him to the hotel, much less return to the Coliseum the next night for another three-hour concert.

Springsteen's devotion to his craft suggests that he has a workaholic syndrome. Bruce often describes what he does as a job, perhaps a reminder of the work and dedication involved. A friend once drew an athletic metaphor in describing how Bruce approaches his art: "You've got two guys with natural talents. Bruce is the guy who respects his talent. He's always in shape, constantly in training—as opposed to the guy next to him who knows he's good and talented but doesn't mind coasting, and who counts on his innate ability a little too much, doesn't realize how much work he's got to put into it."

Some of those around Springsteen notice a loosening up, however.

"Everything about him tells me he's happier now than any time since I met him," one Springsteen ally said after the Greensboro concert. "He has so much confidence about the work he is doing right now that he is able to increase the time he spends on his personal life. It means he doesn't have to do this twenty-four hours a day any longer."

As we chatted, I thought again about the question of sacrifice, and

Left: Bruce unwinds backstage despite a security breach by costumed Kodiak bear. Below: Bussing a fan.

asked Bruce how he has been able to maintain this high sense of dedication for so long.

He was silent for a moment. He looked at me, then at the ground. For all his reluctance to do interviews, he works hard at giving clear, helpful answers, and he seemed frustrated over being unable to find a concise answer to this question.

"I don't know the answer to that question," he finally said, almost apologetically. "That question—how long can I do this—is something I used to ask myself, and then I woke up one day and I said, 'Oh, wait a minute, I know who I am... I'm the guy who does this.'

"I know I'm not making it very clear. But it's not a very clear thing. It's just something I really don't know. I don't know how we play that long... I don't know how my voice holds out that long. I don't know."

Before he could finish the sentence, I asked him another question. I felt like an attorney pumping questions at a man on the witness stand.

"I don't think I felt I was making any sacrifices until I was older—until probably relatively recently when I see George [Theiss] or the friend who was on stage tonight who was in Steel Mill [Robin Thompson]. Robin's married and has three kids and everything. In the early years, I was just doing what came natural. But I do think about it now. There are unreasonable demands made upon you in this business, and at the same time there are unreasonable rewards that you get also. You get a tremendous amount of people's affection, sincere affection."

One area that this unusually open artist keeps to himself is his love life, but even he has joked about his "roadrunner" relationship with women. The term doesn't refer to constant affairs on the road, but to the fact that he is believed to have had only two relationships that lasted more than a year. Doesn't he feel the need for a relationship?

"Everybody feels that all the time," he said, without hesitation. "I guess relationships have been [hard for me] just because I've traveled for my whole adult life, and it was difficult to settle into something and make those types of sacrifices... I guess the most precious thing anybody has in the end is their time.

"That's what you can't bargain with... and you never know when it is going to run out. I've changed quite a bit. It's not a question of wanting to do less. It's just more a question of wanting to round out your life."

Months later—just after midnight on May 13, 1985 at a Roman Catholic Church in Lake Oswego, Oregon—Springsteen married Julianne Phillips, a 25-year-old actress whom he had met backstage after a concert seven months before at the Los Angeles Sports Arena. Phillips, youngest of six children, had appeared in three TV movies, including "His Mistress" and "Summer Fantasy."

Bruce's family and friends were delighted. "We're all thrilled," his

Julianne Phillips. As fans converged on Lake Oswego, Oregon, she and Bruce moved the wedding ceremony up three days. Grown women wept and the *Asbury Park Press* wrote, "You could almost hear the sound of hearts breaking all along the Jersey Shore."

aunt, Dora Kirby, told me the morning after the news hit the papers. "She's a wonderful girl...just what Bruce needed."

After nearly twenty years of believing there wasn't room for anything except rock & roll in his life, Springsteen finally realized there was a place for something—or someone—else.

Springsteen had obviously thought a lot about this himself lately.

"I think you can make anything happen. That's my approach. To blame something on your job is an excuse, no matter what it is. It can make it difficult, no doubt about it. But in the end, you do what you want to do. That's what I basically believe. All the rest is excuses."

Finally, I switched the topic back to the pressures on his end, the matter of his trying to live up to what Elvis first represented to him.

He looked at me kind of skeptically. He wasn't sure about this Elvis comparison. He seemed to be squirming a bit on the stand.

"I think about Elvis a lot and what happened to him," he said finally. "The demands that this profession make on you are unreasonable. It's very strange to go out and have people look at you like you're Santa Claus or the Easter Bunny.

"It's a confusing experience for them, too. Who are they meeting? They're not quite sure. If you don't respond exactly as they imagined or something, which you're not gonna...it can be a strange experience. If you expect it to be a reasonable thing, it can drive you crazy. The answer is trying to stay healthy—mentally, physically, spiritually—all under a lot of pressure."

As an assistant signaled Bruce that the van was ready for the ride to the hotel, I raised the question again about his audience and how he has been able to avoid the isolation that surrounded Elvis. In Greensboro, as elsewhere, he seemed approachable, not a distant pop star.

"That's important because it kind of makes the whole thing more real," Bruce responded. "You want people to see that you are a human being, and you are doing your best under difficult circumstances [laughs], like everybody is. That's one of the things you want to communicate, 'Hey, it's tough, but keep going.'

"It's like giving people hope and giving yourself hope. You have to be a part of your audience in a fashion. You write the song just for yourself, but it's no good unless you play it for somebody else. That's the connection between people that is forever lasting and can never be broken apart."

Before leaving, Springsteen considered a final question. What about the faith people have in you? Is that a source of strength or is it something that drains you?

"There are times you think about those things, and there are times you don't," Bruce said. "You generally think about them when you have to, when you are confronted with a question or a decision. The rest of the time, you are like a guy just trying to do a good job.

"While you do have the responsibility to do a good job, you don't have a responsibility of carrying 20,000 people's dreams and

Preceding pages: Detroit's own Mitch Ryder, belting out "Devil with a Blue Dress On", one of his white soul hits that influenced Springsteen.

desires. That's their job.

"I do my job and they do theirs, and there is a place where you come together and support each other equally almost in your quest for the things that you want, that you need, the love you are looking for or whatever. That's what the concerts are."

When Springsteen emerged from the dressing room, a couple dozen fans and arena employees were waiting. As I've seen him do so often, he stopped to sign autographs and pose for photos. Back at the hotel, some more fans were waiting and he went through the same process again before heading to his room and sleep.

Bruce had reached another plateau. He was the most respected and possibly the most popular rock star in the world. This was the time, ironically, that he should have been on the covers of *Time* and *Newsweek*. But the world rarely works rationally.

Anyone who remembers how Springsteen labored under the "new Bob Dylan tag" in the early '70s would have been intrigued by the scene in A&M's Hollywood recording studios on January 28, 1985. More than forty American pop stars had gathered to record a song—"We Are the World"—as part of a USA for Africa project to raise funds for famine victims.

To maximize the record's appeal, organizers had invited singers representing different areas and styles. The stars ranged from Michael Jackson and Lionel Richie to Willie Nelson and Ray Charles to Bette Midler and Cyndi Lauper. In the studio, this diversity resulted in a colorful mix of hairstyles and wardrobes.

From the rear of the room, however, two artists looked exactly alike as they stepped to the microphones for their solos. Springsteen and Dylan both wore black leather jackets, black pants and heavy boots. With their dark unkempt hair, they looked like they had just tumbled out of a laundry hamper.

As they began singing their respective lines, however, the differences between these two major rock figures seemed far stronger than their similarities.

Dylan guaranteed rock a future in the '60s when he demonstrated that the music was a vital form of artistic expression. Springsteen hasn't revolutionized rock songwriting, yet he has made arguably as vital a contribution to the rock tradition by giving people something and someone to believe in.

It isn't a matter of bigger or best when analyzing Dylan or Springsteen or Presley or Little Richard. Despite the temptation to link artists musically, greatness always asserts its own identity. Dylan did exactly what was necessary in an era when rock's artistry was in question. Springsteen played the same essential role in a time when rock's heart was in doubt.

It was dawn when Springsteen left the studio. While most of the artists who had participated in the session stepped into waiting limousines, Bruce walked through the A&M gates toward his car, which he had parked up the street. When an A&M security guard asked if he wanted an escort, Springsteen just smiled. "No, thanks. I can make it on my own."

Catholic school girls crowd Bruce's van in Philadelphia, 1984.

CREDITS

Jeff Albertson (Page 65); Asbury Park *Press* (19, 22-23, 70-71); *Backstreets* magazine (27); Larry Busacca (6-7, 11, 16-17, 18, 20-21, 24, 28, 183, 218-219, 238-239); Peter Cunningham (24, 31, 37, 42-43, 45, 47, 50, 55, 59, 62-63, 66, 69, 72, 83, 85, 87); Ben DeSoto (129, 130-131); Felix Photography/B.L. Howard Productions, Ltd. (140-141, 146-147, 166-167, 192-193); David Gahr (33, 34-35, 38, 39, 88-89, 40-41, 44, 51, 56-57, 60, 76, 77, 78, 80, 88-89, 93, 94-95, 96-97, 108-109, 113, 118, 144, 178-179, 188-189, 202-203, 205, 223, 226-227, 234-235); Barry Goldenberg (75, 91, 132-133, 134, 135, 136, 169, 177, 196-197, 198-199, 204, 211); Howard B. Leibowitz/B.L. Howard Productions, Ltd. (8, 84, 116, 117, 206); Laura Levine (174-175, 220-221, 228-229, 242-243, 246-247); Ross Marino (119, 158, 191, 230-231, 232-233, 244-245, 250-251); Jeffrey Mayer (173, Cover photograph); Laurie Paladino (139, 180-181, 195, 208-209, 216-217, 224, 248-249); Bob Sorce/Pix Int'l (152); Neal Preston (240, 215 Back cover photograph); Aaron Rapaport (201); RETNA: Michael Putland/RETNA Ltd. (53), Trix von Dugteren/RETNA Ltd. (145), Chris Walter/RETNA Ltd. (148-149), Daryll Pitt/RETNA Ltd. (170-171, 187), Gary Gershoff/RETNA Ltd. (212-213); Ebet Roberts (157, 186, 190); James Shive (125); Bob Sorce (112); STARFILE: Anastasia Pantsios/STARFILE (103, 114-115, 120, 124, 126-127, 159, 172, 210, 252-253), Bob Gruen/STARFILE (106-107, 142-143), Paul Natkin/STARFILE (184-185); Frank Stefanko (15, 98, 99, 100-101, 110, 111, 150-151, 154-155, 160, 162-163, 164, 165); THUNDER THUMBS: Richard E. Aaron/THUNDER THUMBS (48-49, 104-105, 123), Dean Messina/THUNDER THUMBS (79, 254, 256); Bob Zimmerman (79, 254, 256).